Squirrels and Other Fur-Bearers

John Burroughs

Contents

SQUIRRELS AND OTHER FUR-BEARERS

BY

John Burroughs

I
SQUIRRELS

Walking through the early October woods one day, I came upon a place where the ground was thickly strewn with very large unopened chestnut burrs. On examination I found that every burr had been cut square off with about an inch of the stem adhering, and not one had been left on the tree. It was not accident, then, but design. Whose design? A squirrel's. The fruit was the finest I had ever seen in the woods, and some wise squirrel had marked it for his own. The burrs were ripe, and had just begun to divide. The squirrel that had taken all this pains had evidently reasoned with himself thus: "Now, these are extremely fine chestnuts, and I want them; if I wait till the burrs open on the tree, the crows and jays will be sure to carry off a great many of the nuts before they fall; then, after the wind has rattled out what remain, there are the mice, the chipmunks, the red squirrels, the raccoons, the grouse, to say nothing of the boys and the pigs, to come in for their share; so I will forestall events a little: I will cut off the burrs when they have matured, and a few days of this dry October weather will cause every one of them to open on the ground; I shall be on hand in the nick of time to gather up my nuts." The squirrel, of course, had to take the chances of a prowler like myself coming along, but he had fairly stolen a march on his neighbors. As I proceeded to collect and open the burrs, I was half prepared to hear an audible protest from the trees about, for I constantly fancied myself watched by shy but jealous eyes. It is an interesting inquiry how the squirrel knew the burrs would open if left to lie on the ground a few days. Perhaps he did not know, but thought the experiment worth trying.

One reason, doubtless, why squirrels are so bold and reckless in leaping through the trees is that, if they miss their hold and fall, they sustain no injury. Every species of tree-squirrel seems to be capable of a sort of rudimentary flying,--at least of making itself into a parachute, so as to ease or break a fall or a leap from a great height. The so-called flying squirrel does this the most perfectly. It opens its furry vestments, leaps into the air, and sails down the steep incline from the top of one tree to the foot of the next as lightly as a bird. But other squirrels know the same trick, only their coat-skirts are not so broad. One day my dog treed a red squirrel in a tall hickory that stood in a meadow on the side of a steep hill. To see what the squirrel would do when closely pressed, I climbed the tree. As I drew near he took refuge in the topmost branch, and then, as I came on, he boldly leaped into the air, spread himself out upon it, and, with a quick, tremulous motion of his tail and legs, descended quite slowly and landed upon the ground thirty feet below me, apparently none the worse for the leap, for he ran with great speed and eluding the dog took refuge in another tree.

A recent American traveler in Mexico gives a still more striking instance of this power of squirrels partially to neutralize the force of gravity when leaping or falling through the air. Some boys had caught a Mexican black squirrel, nearly as large as a cat. It had escaped from them once, and, when pursued, had taken a leap of sixty feet, from the top of a pine-tree down upon the roof of a house, without injury. This feat had led the grandmother of one of the boys to declare that the squirrel was bewitched, and the boys proposed to put the matter to further test by throwing the squirrel down a precipice six hundred feet high. Our traveler interfered, to see that the squirrel had fair play. The prisoner was conveyed in a pillow-slip to the edge of the cliff, and the slip opened, so that he might have his choice, whether to remain a captive or to take the leap. He looked down the awful abyss, and then back and sidewise,--his eyes glistening, his form crouching. Seeing no escape in any other direction, "he took a flying leap into space, and fluttered rather than fell into the abyss below. His legs began to work like those of a swimming poodle-dog, but quicker and quicker, while his tail, slightly elevated, spread out like a feather fan. A rabbit of the same weight would have made the trip in about twelve seconds; the squirrel protracted it for more than half a minute," and "landed on a ledge of limestone, where we could see him plainly squat on his hind legs and smooth his ruffled fur, after which he made for the creek with a flourish of his tail, took a good drink, and scampered away into the willow thicket."

The story at first blush seems incredible, but I have no doubt our red squirrel would have made the leap safely; then why not the great black squirrel, since its parachute would be proportionately large?

The tails of the squirrels are broad and long and flat, not short and small like those of gophers, chipmunks, woodchucks, and other ground rodents, and when they leap or fall through the air the tail is arched and rapidly vibrates. A squirrel's tail, therefore, is something more than ornament, something more than a flag; it not only aids him in flying, but it serves as a cloak, which he wraps about him when he sleeps.

In making the flying leap I have described the animals' legs are widely extended, their bodies broadened and flattened, the tail stiffened and slightly curved, and a curious tremulous motion runs through all. It is very obvious that a deliberate attempt is made to present the broadest surface possible to the air, and I think a red squirrel might leap from almost any height to the ground without serious injury. Our flying squirrel is in no proper sense a flyer. On the ground he is more helpless than a chipmunk, because less agile. He can only sail or slide down a steep incline from the top of one tree to the foot of another. The flying squirrel is active only at night; hence its large, soft eyes, its soft fur, and its gentle, shrinking ways. It is the gentlest and most harmless of our rodents. A pair of them for two or three successive years had their nest behind the blinds of an upper window of a large, unoccupied country-house near me. You could stand in the room inside and observe the happy family through the window pane against which their nest pressed. There on the window sill lay a pile of large, shining chestnuts, which they were evidently holding against a time of scarcity, as the pile did not diminish while I observed them. The nest was composed of cotton and wool which they filched from a bed in one of the chambers, and it was always a mystery how they got into the room to obtain it. There seemed to be no other avenue but the chimney flue.

Red and gray squirrels are more or less active all winter, though very shy, and, I am inclined to think, partially nocturnal in their habits. Here a gray one has just passed,--came down that tree and went up this; there he dug for a beechnut, and left the burr on the snow. How did he know where to dig? During an unusually severe winter I have known him to make long journeys to a barn, in a remote field, where wheat was stored. How did he know there was wheat there? In attempting to return, the adventurous creature was frequently run down and caught in the deep snow.

His home is in the trunk of some old birch or maple, with an entrance far up amid the branches. In the spring he builds himself a summer-house of small leafy twigs in the top of a neighboring beech, where the young are reared and much of the time passed. But the safer retreat in the maple is not abandoned, and both old and young resort thither in the fall, or when danger threatens. Whether this temporary residence amid the branches is for elegance or pleasure, or for sanitary reasons or domestic convenience, the naturalist has forgotten to mention.

The elegant creature, so cleanly in its habits, so graceful in its carriage, so nimble and daring in its movements, excites feelings of admiration akin to those awakened by the birds and the fairer forms of nature. His passage through the trees is almost a flight. Indeed, the flying squirrel has little or no advantage over him, and in speed and nimbleness cannot compare with him at all. If he miss his footing and fall, he is sure to catch on the next branch; if the connection be broken, he leaps recklessly for the nearest spray or limb, and secures his hold, even if it be by the aid of his teeth.

His career of frolic and festivity begins in the fall, after the birds have left us and the holiday spirit of nature has commenced to subside. How much his presence adds to the pleasure of a saunter in the still October woods. You step lightly across the threshold of the forest, and sit down upon the first log or rock to await the signals. It is so still that the ear suddenly seems to have acquired new powers, and there is no movement to confuse the eye. Presently you hear the rustling of a branch, and see it sway or spring as the squirrel leaps from or to it; or else you hear a disturbance in the dry leaves, and mark one running upon the ground. He has probably seen the intruder, and, not liking his stealthy movements, desires to avoid a nearer acquaintance. Now he mounts a stump to see if the way is clear, then pauses a moment at the foot of a tree to take his bearings, his tail as he skims along undulating behind him, and adding to the easy grace and dignity of his movements. Or else you are first advised of his proximity by the dropping of a false nut, or the fragments of the shucks rattling upon the leaves. Or, again, after contemplating you a while unobserved, and making up his mind that you are not dangerous, he strikes an attitude on a branch, and commences to quack and bark, with an accompanying movement of his tail. Late in the afternoon, when the same stillness reigns, the same scenes are repeated. There is a black variety, quite rare, but mating freely with the gray, from which it seems to be distinguished only in color.

The red squirrel is more common and less dignified than the gray, and oftener guilty of petty larceny about the barns and grain-fields. He is most abundant in mixed oak, chestnut, and hemlock woods, from which he makes excursions to the fields and orchards, spinning along the tops of the fences, which afford not only convenient lines of communication, but a safe retreat if danger threatens. He loves to linger about the orchard; and, sitting upright on the topmost stone in the wall, or on the tallest stake in the fence, chipping up an apple for the seeds, his tail conforming to the curve of his back, his paws shifting and turning the apple, he is a pretty sight, and his bright, pert appearance atones for all the mischief he does. At home, in the woods, he is very frolicsome and loquacious. The appearance of anything unusual, if after contemplating it a moment, he concludes it not dangerous, excites his unbounded mirth and ridicule, and he snickers and chatters, hardly able to contain himself; now darting up the trunk of a tree and squealing in derision, then hopping into position on a limb and dancing to the music of his own cackle, and all for your special benefit.

There is something very human in this apparent mirth and mockery of the squirrels. It seems to be a sort of ironical laughter, and implies self-conscious pride and exultation in the laughter. "What a ridiculous thing you are, to be sure!" he seems to say; "how clumsy and awkward, and what a poor show for a tail! Look at me, look at me!"--and he capers about in his best style. Again, he would seem to tease you and provoke your attention; then suddenly assumes a tone of good-natured, childlike defiance and derision. That pretty little imp, the chipmunk, will sit on the stone above his den and defy you, as plainly as if he said so, to catch him before he can get into his hole if you can.

A hard winter affects the chipmunks very little; they are snug and warm in their burrows in the ground and under the rocks, with a bountiful store of nuts or grain. I have heard of nearly a half-bushel of chestnuts being taken from a single den. They usually hole up in November, and do not come out again till March or April, unless the winter is very open and mild. Gray squirrels, when they have been partly domesticated in parks and groves near dwellings, are said to hide their nuts here and there upon the ground, and in winter to dig them up from beneath the snow, always hitting the spot accurately.

The red squirrel lays up no stores like the provident chipmunk, but scours about for food in all weathers, feeding upon the seeds in the cones of the hemlock that still cling to the tree, upon sumac-bobs, and the seeds of frozen apples. I have seen the ground under a wild apple-tree that stood near the woods completely covered with the "chonkings" of the frozen apples, the work of the squirrels in getting at the seeds; not an apple had been left, and apparently not a seed had been lost. But the squirrels in this particular locality evidently got pretty hard up before spring, for they developed a new source of food-supply. A young bushy-topped sugar-maple, about forty feet high, standing beside a stone fence near the woods, was attacked, and more than half denuded of its bark. The object of the squirrels seemed to be to get at the soft, white, mucilaginous substance (cambium layer) between the bark and the wood. The ground was covered with fragments of the bark, and the white, naked stems and branches had been scraped by fine teeth. When the sap starts in the early spring, the squirrels add this to their scanty supplies. They perforate the bark of the branches of the maples with their chisel-like teeth, and suck the sweet liquid as it slowly oozes out. It is not much as food, but evidently it helps.

I have said the red squirrel does not lay by a store of food for winter use, like the chipmunk and the wood-mice; yet in the fall he sometimes hoards in a tentative, temporary kind of way. I have seen his savings--butternuts and black walnuts--stuck here and there in saplings and trees near his nest; sometimes carefully inserted in the upright fork of a limb or twig. One day, late in November, I counted a dozen or more black walnuts put away in this manner in a little grove of locusts, chestnuts, and maples by the roadside, and could but smile at the wise forethought of the rascally squirrel. His supplies were probably safer that way than if more elaborately hidden. They were well distributed; his eggs were not all in one basket, and he could go away from home without any fear that his storehouse would be broken into in his absence. The next week, when I passed that way, the nuts were all gone but two. I saw the squirrel that doubtless laid claim to them, on each occasion.

There is one thing the red squirrel knows unerringly that I do not (there are probably several other things); that is, on which side of the butternut the meat lies. He always gnaws through the shell so as to strike the kernel broadside, and thus easily extract it; while to my eyes there is no external mark or indication, in the form or appearance of the nut, as there is in the hickory-nut, by which I can tell whether the edge or the side of the meat is toward me. But examine any number of nuts that the squirrels have rifled, and, as a rule, you will find they always drill through the shell at the one spot where the meat will be most exposed. Occasionally one makes a mistake, but not often. It stands them in hand to know, and they do know. Doubtless, if butternuts were a main source of my food, and I were compelled to gnaw into them, I should learn, too, on which side my bread was buttered.

The cheeks of the red and gray squirrels are made without pockets, and whatever they transport is carried in the teeth. They are more or less active all winter, but October and November are their festal months. Invade some butternut or hickory grove on a frosty October morning, and hear the red squirrel beat the "juba" on a horizontal branch. It is a most lively jig, what the boys call a "regular break-down," interspersed with squeals and snickers and derisive laughter. The most noticeable peculiarity about the vocal part of it is the fact that it is a kind of duet. In other words, by some ventriloquial tricks, he appears to accompany himself, as if his voice split up, a part forming a low guttural sound, and a part a shrill nasal sound.

II
THE CHIPMUNK

The first chipmunk in March is as sure a token of the spring as the first bluebird or the first robin, and is quite as welcome. Some genial influence has found him out there in his burrow, deep under the ground, and waked him up, and enticed him forth into the light of day. The red squirrel has been more or less active all winter; his track has dotted the surface of every new-fallen snow throughout the season. But the chipmunk retired from view early in December, and has passed the rigorous months in his nest, beside his hoard of nuts, some feet underground, and hence, when he emerges in March, and is seen upon his little journeys along the fences, or perched upon a log or rock near his hole in the woods, it is another sign that spring is at hand. His store of nuts may or may not be all consumed; it is certain that he is no sluggard, to sleep away these first bright warm days.

Before the first crocus is out of the ground, you may look for the first chipmunk. When I hear the little downy woodpecker begin his spring drumming, then I know the chipmunk is due. He cannot sleep after that challenge of the woodpecker reaches his ear.

Apparently the first thing he does on coming forth, as soon as he is sure of himself, is to go courting. So far as I have observed, the love-making of the chipmunk occurs in March. A single female will attract all the males in the vicinity. One early March day I was at work for several hours near a stone fence, where a female had apparently taken up her quarters. What a train of suitors she had that day! how they hurried up and down, often giving each other a spiteful slap or bite as they passed. The young are born in May, four or five at a birth.

The chipmunk is quite a solitary creature; I have never known more than one to occupy the same den. Apparently no two can agree to live together. What a clean, pert, dapper, nervous little fellow he is! How fast his heart beats, as he stands up on the wall by the roadside, and, with hands spread out upon his breast, regards you intently! A movement of your arm, and he darts into the wall with a saucy *chip-r-r*, which has the effect of slamming the door behind him.

On some still day in autumn, one of the nutty days, the woods will often be pervaded by an undertone of sound, produced by their multitudinous clucking, as they sit near their dens. It is one of the characteristic sounds of fall.

I was much amused one October in watching a chipmunk carry nuts and other food into his den. He had made a well-defined path from his door out through the weeds and dry leaves into the territory where his feeding-ground lay. The path was a crooked one; it dipped under weeds, under some large, loosely piled stones, under a pile of chestnut posts, and then followed the remains of an old wall. Going and coming, his motions were like clock-work. He always went by spurts and sudden sallies. He was never for one moment off his guard. He would appear at the mouth of his den, look quickly about, take a few leaps to a tussock of grass, pause a breath with one foot raised, slip quickly a few yards over some dry leaves, pause again by a stump beside a path, rush across the path to the pile of loose stones, go under the first and over the second, gain the pile of posts, make his way through that, survey his course a half moment from the other side of it, and then dart on to some other cover, and presently beyond my range, where I think he gathered acorns, as there were no other nut-bearing trees than oaks near. In four or five minutes I would see him coming back, always keeping rigidly to the course he took going out, pausing at the same spots, darting over or under the same objects, clearing at a bound the same pile of leaves. There was no variation in his manner of proceeding all the time I observed him.

He was alert, cautious, and exceedingly methodical. He had found safety in a certain course, and he did not at any time deviate a hair's breadth from it. Something seemed to say to him all the time, "Beware, beware!" The nervous, impetuous ways of these creatures are no doubt the result of the life of fear which they lead.

My chipmunk had no companion. He lived all by himself in true hermit fashion, as is usually the case with this squirrel. Provident creature that he is, one would think that he would long ago have discovered that heat, and therefore food, is economized by two or three nesting together.

One day in early spring, a chipmunk that lived near me met with a terrible adventure, the memory of which will probably be handed down through many generations of its family. I was sitting in the summer-house with Nig the cat upon my knee, when the chipmunk came out of its den a few feet away, and ran quickly to a pile of chestnut posts about twenty yards from where I sat. Nig saw it, and was off my lap upon the floor in an instant. I spoke sharply to the cat, when she sat down and folded her paws under her, and regarded the squirrel, as I thought, with only a dreamy kind of interest. I fancied she thought it a hopeless case there amid that pile of posts. "That is not your game, Nig," I said, "so spare yourself any anxiety." Just then I was called to the house, where I was detained about five minutes. As I returned I met Nig coming to the house with the chipmunk in her mouth. She had the air of one who had won a wager. She carried the chipmunk by the throat, and its body hung limp from her mouth. I quickly took the squirrel from her, and reproved her sharply. It lay in my hand as if dead, though I saw no marks of the cat's teeth upon it. Presently it gasped for its breath, then again and again. I saw that the cat had simply choked it. Quickly the film passed off its eyes, its heart began visibly to beat, and slowly the breathing became regular. I carried it back, and laid it down in the door of its den. In a moment it crawled or kicked itself in. In the afternoon I placed a handful of corn there, to express my sympathy, and as far as possible make amends for Nig's cruel treatment.

Not till four or five days had passed did my little neighbor emerge again from its den, and then only for a moment. That terrible black monster with the large green-yellow eyes,--it might be still lurking near. How the black monster had captured the alert and restless squirrel so quickly, under the circumstances, was a great mystery to me. Was not its eye as sharp as the cat's, and its movements as quick? Yet cats do have the secret of catching squirrels, and birds, and mice, but I have never yet had the luck to see it done.

It was not very long before the chipmunk was going to and from her den as usual, though the dread of the black monster seemed ever before her, and gave speed and extra alertness to all her movements. In early summer four young chipmunks emerged from the den, and ran freely about. There was nothing to disturb them, for, alas! Nig herself was now dead.

One summer day I watched a cat for nearly a half hour trying her arts upon a chipmunk that sat upon a pile of stone. Evidently her game was to stalk him. She had cleared half the distance, or about twelve feet, that separated the chipmunk from a dense Norway spruce, when I chanced to become a spectator of the little drama. There sat the cat crouched low on the grass, her big, yellow eyes fixed upon the chipmunk, and there sat the chipmunk at the mouth of his den, motionless, with his eyes fixed upon the cat. For a long time neither moved. "Will the cat bind him with her fatal spell?" I thought. Sometimes her head slowly lowered and her eyes seemed to dilate, and I fancied she was about to spring. But she did not. The distance was too great to be successfully cleared in one bound. Then the squirrel moved nervously, but kept his eye upon the enemy. Then the cat evidently grew tired and relaxed a little and looked behind her. Then she crouched again and riveted her gaze upon the squirrel. But the latter would not be hypnotized; he shifted his position a few times and finally quickly entered his den, when the cat soon slunk away.

In digging his hole it is evident that the chipmunk carries away the loose soil. Never a grain of it is seen in front of his door. Those pockets of his probably stand him in good stead on such occasions. Only in one instance have I seen a pile of earth before the entrance to a chipmunk's den, and that was where the builder had begun his house late in November, and was probably too much hurried to remove this ugly mark from before his door. I used to pass his place every morning in my walk, and my eye always fell upon that little pile of red, freshly-dug soil. A little later I used frequently to surprise the squirrel furnishing his house, carrying in dry leaves of the maple and plane tree. He would seize a large leaf and with both hands stuff it into his cheek pockets, and then carry it into his den. I saw him on several different days occupied in this way. I trust he had secured his winter stores, though I am a little doubtful. He was hurriedly making himself a new home, and the cold of December was upon us while he was yet at work. It may be that he had moved the stores from his old quarters, wherever they were, and again it may be that he had been dispossessed of both his house and provender by some other chipmunk.

I have been told by a man who says he has seen what he avers, that the reason why we do not find a pile of fresh earth beside the hole of the chipmunk is this: In making his den the workman continues his course through the soil a foot or more under the surface for several yards, carrying out the earth in his cheek pouches and dumping it near the entrance. Then he comes to the surface and makes a new hole from beneath, which is, of course, many feet from the first hole. This latter is now closed up, and henceforth the new one alone is used. I have no doubt this is the true explanation.

When nuts or grain are not to be had, these thrifty little creatures will find some substitute to help them over the winter. Two chipmunks near my study were occupied many days in carrying in cherry pits which they gathered beneath a large cherry-tree that stood ten or twelve rods away. As Nig was no longer about to molest them, they grew very fearless, and used to spin up and down the garden path to and from their source of supplies in a way quite unusual with these timid creatures. After they had got enough cherry pits, they gathered the seed of a sugar maple that stood near. Many of the keys remained upon the tree after the leaves had fallen, and these the squirrels harvested. They would run swiftly out upon the ends of the small branches, reach out for the maple keys, snip off the wings, and deftly slip the nut or samara into their cheek pockets. Day after day in late autumn, I used to see them thus occupied.

As I have said, I have no evidence that more than one chipmunk occupy the same den. One March morning after a light fall of snow I saw where one had come up out of his hole, which was in the side of our path to the vineyard, and after a moment's survey of the surroundings had started off on his travels. I followed the track to see where he had gone. He had passed through my woodpile, then under the beehives, then around the study and under some spruces and along the slope to the hole of a friend of his, about sixty yards from his own. Apparently he had gone in here, and then his friend had come forth with him, for there were two tracks leading from this doorway. I followed them to a third humble entrance, not far off, where the tracks were so numerous that I lost the trail. It was pleasing to see the evidence of their morning sociability written there upon the new snow.

One of the enemies of the chipmunk, as I discovered lately, is the weasel. I was sitting in the woods one autumn day when I heard a small cry, and a rustling amid the branches of a tree a few rods beyond me. Looking thither I saw a chipmunk fall through the air, and catch on a limb twenty or more feet from the ground. He appeared to have dropped from near the top of the tree.

He secured his hold upon the small branch that had luckily intercepted his fall, and sat perfectly still. In a moment more I saw a weasel--one of the smaller red varieties--come down the trunk of the tree, and begin exploring the branches on a level with the chipmunk.

I saw in a moment what had happened. The weasel had driven the squirrel from his retreat in the rocks and stones beneath, and had pressed him so closely that he had taken refuge in the top of a tree. But weasels can climb trees, too, and this one had tracked the frightened chipmunk to the topmost branch, where he had tried to seize him. Then the squirrel had, in horror, let go his hold, screamed, and fallen through the air, till he struck the branch as just described. Now his blood-thirsty enemy was looking for him again, apparently relying entirely upon his sense of smell to guide him to the game.

How did the weasel know the squirrel had not fallen clear to the ground? He certainly did know, for when he reached the same tier of branches he began exploring them. The chipmunk sat transfixed with fear, frozen with terror, not twelve feet away, and yet the weasel saw him not.

Round and round, up and down, he went on the branches, exploring them over and over. How he hurried, lest the trail get cold! How subtle and cruel and fiendish he looked! His snakelike movements, his tenacity, his speed!

He seemed baffled; he knew his game was near, but he could not strike the spot. The branch, upon the extreme end of which the squirrel sat, ran out and up from the tree seven or eight feet, and then, turning a sharp elbow, swept down and out at right angles with its first course.

The weasel would pause each time at this elbow and turn back. It seemed as if he knew that particular branch held his prey, and yet its crookedness each time threw him out. He would not give it up, but went over his course again and again.

One can fancy the feelings of the chipmunk, sitting there in plain view a few feet away, watching his deadly enemy hunting for the clue. How his little heart must have fairly stood still each time the fatal branch was struck! Probably as a last resort he would again have let go his hold and fallen to the ground, where he might have eluded his enemy a while longer.

In the course of five or six minutes the weasel gave over the search, and ran hurriedly down the tree to the ground. The chipmunk remained motionless for a long time; then he stirred a little as if hope were reviving. Then he looked nervously about him; then he had recovered himself so far as to change his position. Presently he began to move cautiously along the branch to the bole of the tree; then, after a few moments' delay, he plucked up courage to descend to the ground, where I hope no weasel has disturbed him since.

One season a chipmunk had his den in the side of the terrace above my garden, and spent the mornings laying in a store of corn which he stole from a field ten or twelve rods away. In traversing about half this distance, the little poacher was exposed; the first cover on the way from his den was a large maple, where he always brought up and took a survey of the scene. I would see him spinning along toward the maple, then from it by an easy stage to the fence adjoining the corn; then back again with his booty. One morning I paused to watch him more at my leisure. He came up out of his retreat and cocked himself up to see what my motions meant. His forepaws were clasped to his breast precisely as if they had been hands, and the tips of the fingers thrust into his vest pockets. Having satisfied himself with reference to me, he sped on toward the tree. He had nearly reached it, when he turned tail and rushed for his hole with the greatest precipitation. As he neared it, I saw some bluish object in the air closing in upon him with the speed of an arrow, and, as he vanished within, a shrike brought up in front of the spot, and with spread wings and tail stood hovering a moment, and, looking in, then turned and went away. Apparently it was a narrow escape for the chipmunk, and, I venture to say, he stole no more corn that morning. The shrike is said to catch mice, but it is not known to attack squirrels. The bird certainly could not have strangled the chipmunk, and I am curious to know what would have been the result had he overtaken him. Probably it was only a kind of brag on his part--a bold dash where no risk was run. He simulated the hawk, the squirrel's real enemy, and no doubt enjoyed the joke.

The sylvan folk seem to know when you are on a peaceful mission, and are less afraid than usual. Did not that marmot to-day guess my errand did not concern him as he saw me approach there from his cover in the bushes? But, when he saw me pause and deliberately seat myself on the stone wall immediately over his hole, his confidence was much shaken. He apparently deliberated awhile, for I heard the leaves rustle as if he were making up his mind, when he suddenly broke cover and came for his hole full tilt. Any other animal would have taken to his heels and fled;

but a woodchuck's heels do not amount to much for speed, and he feels his only safety is in his hole. On he came in the most obstinate and determined manner, and I dare say if I had sat down in his hole would have attacked me unhesitatingly. This I did not give him a chance to do, and he whipped into his den beneath me with a defiant snort. Farther on, a saucy chipmunk presumed upon my harmless character to an unwonted degree also. I had paused to bathe my hands and face in a little trout brook, and had set a tin cup, which I had partly filled with strawberries as I crossed the field, on a stone at my feet, when along came the chipmunk as confidently as if he knew precisely where he was going, and, perfectly oblivious of my presence, cocked himself up on the rim of the cup and proceeded to eat my choicest berries. I remained motionless and observed him. He had eaten but two when the thought seemed to occur to him that he might be doing better, and he began to fill his pockets. Two, four, six, eight of my berries quickly disappeared, and the cheeks of the little vagabond swelled. But all the time he kept eating, that not a moment might be lost. Then he hopped off the cup, and went skipping from stone to stone till the brook was passed, when he disappeared in the woods. In two or three minutes he was back again, and went to stuffing himself as before; then he disappeared a second time, and I imagined told a friend of his, for in a moment or two along came a bob-tailed chipmunk, as if in search of something, and passed up, and down, and around, but did not quite hit the spot. Shortly, the first returned a third time, and had now grown a little fastidious, for he began to sort over my berries, and to bite into them, as if to taste their quality. He was not long in loading up, however, and in making off again. But I had now got tired of the joke, and my berries were appreciably diminishing, so I moved away. What was most curious about the proceeding was, that the little poacher took different directions each time, and returned from different ways. Was this to elude pursuit, or was he distributing the fruit to his friends and neighbors about, astonishing them with strawberries for lunch?

On another occasion I was much amused by three chipmunks, who seemed to be engaged in some kind of game. It looked very much as if they were playing tag. Round and round they would go, first one taking the lead, then another, all good-natured and gleeful as schoolboys. There is one thing about a chipmunk that is peculiar: he is never more than one jump from home. Make a dive at him anywhere and in he goes. He knows where the hole is, even when it is covered up with leaves.

There is no doubt, also, that he has his own sense of humor and fun, as what squirrel has not? I have watched two red squirrels for a half hour coursing through the large trees by the roadside where branches interlocked, and engaged in a game of tag as obviously as two boys. As soon as the pursuer had come up with the pursued, and actually touched him, the palm was his, and away he would go, taxing his wits and his speed to the utmost to elude his fellow.

I have observed that any unusual disturbance in the woods, near where the chipmunk has his den, will cause him to shift his quarters. One October, for many successive days, I saw one carrying into his hole buckwheat which he had stolen from a near field. The hole was only a few rods from where we were getting out stone, and as our work progressed, and the racket and uproar increased, the chipmunk became alarmed. He ceased carrying in, and after much hesitating and darting about, and some prolonged absences, he began to carry out; he had determined to move; if the mountain fell, he, at least, would be away in time. So, by mouthfuls or cheekfuls, the grain was transferred to a new place. He did not make a "bee" to get it done, but carried it all himself, occupying several days, and making a trip about every ten minutes.

III
THE WOODCHUCK

In the Middle and Eastern States our woodchuck takes the place, in some respects, of the English rabbit, burrowing in every hillside and under every stone wall and jutting ledge and large boulder, whence it makes raids upon the grass and clover and sometimes upon the garden vegetables. It is quite solitary in its habits, seldom more than one inhabiting the same den, unless it be a mother and her young. It is not now so much a *wood* chuck as a *field* chuck. Occasionally, however, one seems to prefer the woods, and is not seduced by the sunny slopes and the succulent grass, but feeds, as did his fathers before him, upon roots and twigs, the bark of young trees, and upon various wood plants.

One summer day, as I was swimming across a broad, deep pool in the creek in a secluded place in the woods, I saw one of these sylvan chucks amid the rocks but a few feet from the edge of the water where I proposed to touch. He saw my approach, but doubtless took me for some water-fowl, or for some cousin of his of the muskrat tribe; for he went on with his feeding, and regarded me not till I paused within ten feet of him and lifted myself up. Then he did not know me, having, perhaps, never seen Adam in his simplicity, but he twisted his nose around to catch my scent; and the moment he had done so he sprang like a jumping-jack and rushed into his den with the utmost precipitation.

The woodchuck is the true serf among our animals; he belongs to the soil, and savors of it. He is of the earth, earthy. There is generally a decided odor about his dens and lurking places, but it is not at all disagreeable in the clover-scented air; and his shrill whistle, as he takes to his hole or defies the farm dog from the interior of the stone wall, is a pleasant summer sound. In form and movement the woodchuck is not captivating. His body is heavy and flabby. Indeed, such a flaccid, fluid, pouchy carcass I have never before seen. It has absolutely no muscular tension or rigidity, but is as baggy and shaky as a skin filled with water. The legs of the woodchuck are short and stout, and made for digging rather than running. The latter operation he performs by short leaps, his belly scarcely clearing the ground. For a short distance he can make very good time, but he seldom trusts himself far from his hole, and, when surprised in that predicament, makes little effort to escape, but, grating his teeth, looks the danger squarely in the face.

I knew a farmer in New York who had a very large bobtailed churn-dog by the name of Cuff. The farmer kept a large dairy and made a great deal of butter, and it was the business of Cuff to spend nearly the half of each summer day treading the endless round of the churning-machine. During the remainder of the day he had plenty of time to sleep and rest, and sit on his hips and survey the landscape. One day, sitting thus, he discovered a woodchuck about forty rods from the house, on a steep sidehill, feeding about near his hole, which was beneath a large rock. The old dog, forgetting his stiffness, and remembering the fun he had had with woodchucks in his earlier days, started off at his highest speed, vainly hoping to catch this one before he could get to his hole. But the woodchuck, seeing the dog come laboring up the hill, sprang to the mouth of his den, and, when his pursuer was only a few rods off, whistled tauntingly and went in. This occurred several times, the old dog marching up the hill, and then marching down again, having had his labor for his pains.

I suspect that he revolved the subject in his mind while revolving the great wheel of the churning-machine, and that some turn or other brought him a happy thought, for next time he showed himself a strategist. Instead of giving chase to the woodchuck, when first discovered, he crouched down to the ground, and, resting his head on his paws, watched him. The woodchuck kept working away from his hole, lured by the tender clover, but, not unmindful of his safety, lifted himself up on his haunches every few moments and surveyed the approaches. Presently, after the woodchuck had let himself down from one of these attitudes of observation and resumed his feeding, Cuff started swiftly but stealthily up the hill, precisely in the attitude of a cat when she is stalking a bird. When the woodchuck rose up again, Cuff was perfectly motionless and half hid by the grass. When he again resumed his clover, Cuff sped up the hill as before, this time crossing a fence, but in a low place, and so nimbly that he was not discovered. Again the woodchuck was on the outlook, again Cuff was motionless and hugging the ground. As the dog neared his victim he was partially hidden by a swell in the earth, but still the woodchuck from his outlook reported "All right," when Cuff, having not twice as far to run as the chuck, threw all stealthiness aside and rushed directly for the hole. At that moment the woodchuck discovered his danger, and, seeing that it was a race for life, leaped as I never saw marmot leap before. But he was two seconds too late, his retreat was cut off, and the powerful jaws of the old dog closed upon him.

The next season Cuff tried the same tactics again with like success, but when the third woodchuck had taken up his abode at the fatal hole, the old churner's wits and strength had begun to fail him, and he was baffled in each attempt to capture the animal.

The woodchuck usually burrows on a sidehill. This enables him to guard against being drowned out, by making the termination of the hole higher than the entrance. He digs in slantingly for about two or three feet, then makes a sharp upward turn and keeps nearly parallel with the surface of the ground for a distance of eight or ten feet farther, according to the grade. Here he makes his nest and passes the winter, holing up in October or November and coming out again in March or April. This is a long sleep, and is rendered possible only by the amount of fat with which the system has become stored during the summer. The fire of life still burns, but very faintly and slowly, as with the draughts all closed and the ashes heaped up. Respiration is continued, but at longer intervals, and all the vital processes are nearly at a standstill. Dig one out during hibernation (Audubon did so), and you find it a mere inanimate ball, that suffers itself to be moved and rolled about without showing signs of awakening. But bring it in by the fire, and it presently unrolls and opens its eyes, and crawls feebly about, and if left to itself will seek some dark hole or corner, roll itself up again, and resume its former condition.

IV
THE RABBIT AND THE HARE

With us the hare is of the remote northern woods, the rabbit is of the fields and bushy margins of the woods. One retreats before man and civilization, the other follows in their wake. The rabbit is now common in parts of our State (New York) where in my boyhood only the hare was found. The rabbit evidently loves to be neighbor to man and profits by it. Nearly every winter one takes up her abode under my study floor, and when the snow is deep and the weather is cold she usually finds every night a couple of sweet apples on her threshold. I suppose she thinks they grow there, or are blown there by the wind like the snow. At such times she does not leave her retreat; the apples are good fortune enough. If I neglect to put them there, in the morning I see where she has gone forth over the lawn looking for them, or for some other food.

I wonder if that fox chanced to catch a glimpse of her the other night when he stealthily leaped over the fence near by and walked along between the study and the house? How clearly one could read that it was not a little dog that had passed there! There was something furtive in the track; it shied off away from the house and around it, as if eyeing it suspiciously; and then it had the caution and deliberation of the fox,--bold, bold, but not too bold; wariness was in every footprint. If it had been a little dog that had chanced to wander that way, when he crossed my path he would have followed it up to the barn and have gone smelling around for a bone; but this sharp, cautious track held straight across all others, keeping five or six rods from the house, up the hill, across the highway toward a neighboring farmstead, with its nose in the air, and its eye and ear alert, so to speak.

One summer a wild rabbit came up within a few feet of my neighbor's house, scooped out a little place in the turf, and reared her family there. I suppose she felt more secure from prowling cats and dogs than in the garden or vineyard. My neighbor took me out to let me into her secret. He pointed down to the ground a few feet in front of us and said, "There it is." I looked and saw nothing but the newly mown turf with one spot the size of my two hands where the grass was apparently dead. "I see no rabbit nor any signs of a rabbit," I replied. He stooped to this dry spot and lifted up a little blanket or carpet of matted dry grass and revealed one of the prettiest sights I had ever seen, and the only one of the kind I had ever looked upon!--four or five little rabbits half the size of chipmunks, cuddled down in a dry fur-lined nest. They did not move or wink, and their ears were pressed down close to their heads. My neighbor let the coverlet fall back, and they were hidden again as by magic.

They had been discovered a few days before when the lawn was mown, and one, as it sprang out from the nest, was killed by the mower, who mistook it for a young rat. The rest of them fled and disappeared through the grass, but the next morning they were back in the nest, where they remained for several days longer. Only at night, so far as was observed, did the mother visit and nurse them.

There was no opening into the nest, the mat of dried grass covered it completely, so that the mother, in her visits to them, must have lifted it up and crept beneath. It was a very pretty and cunning device. One might have stepped upon it in his walk, but surely his eyes alone would never have penetrated the secret. I am told by men wise in the lore of the fields and woods that the rabbit always covers her nest and young with a little blanket, usually made of fur plucked from her own breast.

The rabbit seems to suffer very little from the deep snows and severe cold of winter. The deeper the snow, the nearer she is brought to the tops of the tender bushes and shoots. I see in my walks where she has cropped the tops of the small, bushy, soft maples, cutting them slantingly as you would with a knife, and quite as smoothly. Indeed, the mark was so like that of a knife that, notwithstanding the tracks, it was only after the closest scrutiny that I was convinced it was the sharp, chisel-like teeth of the rabbit. She leaves no chips, and apparently makes clean work of every twig she cuts off.

The hare is nocturnal in its habits, and though a very lively creature at night, with regular courses and run-ways through the wood, is entirely quiet by day.

Timid as he is, he makes little effort to conceal himself, usually squatting beside a log, stump, or tree, and seeming to avoid rocks and ledges where he might be partially housed from the cold and the snow, but where also--and this consideration undoubtedly determines his choice--he would be more apt to fall a prey to his enemies. In this, as well as in many other respects, he differs from the rabbit proper. He never burrows in the ground, or takes refuge in a den or hole, when pursued. If caught in the open fields, he is much confused and easily overtaken by the dog; but in the woods, he leaves his enemy at a bound. In summer, when first disturbed, he beats the ground violently with his feet, by which means he would express to you his surprise or displeasure; it is a dumb way he has of scolding. After leaping a few yards, he pauses an instant, as if to determine the degree of danger, and then hurries away with a much lighter tread.

His feet are like great pads, and his track in the snow has little of the sharp, articulated expression of Reynard's, or of animals that climb or dig. Yet it is very pretty, like all the rest, and tells its own tale. There is nothing bold or vicious or vulpine in it, and his timid, harmless character is published at every leap. He abounds in dense woods, preferring localities filled with a small undergrowth of beech and birch, upon the bark of which he feeds. Nature is rather partial to him, and matches his extreme local habits and character with a suit that corresponds with his surroundings,--reddish gray in summer and white in winter.

V
THE MUSKRAT

It sometimes looks as if the muskrat were weather-wise and could forecast the coming season. I doubt if a long series of observations would bear out the truth of this remark, yet I have noticed that in his nest-building he sometimes hits the mark with surprising accuracy.

In the fall of 1878 I observed that he built unusually high and massive nests. I noticed them in several different localities. In a shallow, sluggish pond by the roadside, which I used to pass daily in my walk, two nests were in process of construction throughout the month of November. The builders worked only at night, and I could see each day that the work had visibly advanced. When there was a slight skim of ice over the pond, this was broken up about the nests, with trails through it in different directions where the material had been brought. The houses were placed a little to one side of the main channel, and were constructed entirely of a species of coarse wild grass that grew all about. So far as I could see, from first to last they were solid masses of grass, as if the interior cavity or nest was to be excavated afterward, as doubtless it was. As they emerged from the pond they gradually assumed the shape of a miniature mountain, very bold and steep on the south side, and running down a long gentle grade to the surface of the water on the north. One could see that the little architect hauled all his material up this easy slope, and thrust it out boldly around the other side. Every mouthful was distinctly defined. After they were two feet or more above the water, I expected each day to see that the finishing stroke had been given and the work brought to a close. But higher yet, said the builder.

December drew near, the cold became threatening, and I was apprehensive that winter would suddenly shut down upon those unfinished nests. But the wise muskrats seemed to know better than I did. Finally, about the 6th of December, the nests assumed completion; the northern incline was absorbed or carried up, and each structure became a strong massive cone, three or four feet high, the largest nest of the kind I had ever seen. "Does it mean a severe winter?" I inquired. An old farmer said it meant "high water," and he was right once, at least, for in a few days afterward we had the heaviest rainfall known in this section for half a century. The creeks rose to an almost unprecedented height. The sluggish pond became a seething, turbulent watercourse; gradually the angry element crept up the sides of these lake dwellings, till, when the rain ceased, about four o'clock, they showed above the flood no larger than a man's hat. During the night the channel shifted till the main current swept over them, and next day not a vestige of the nests was to be seen; they had gone downstream, as had many other dwellings of a less temporary character. The rats had built wisely, and would have been perfectly secure against any ordinary high water, but who can foresee a flood? The oldest traditions of their race did not run back to the time of such a visitation.

Nearly a week afterward another dwelling was begun, well away from the treacherous channel, but the architects did not work at it with much heart; the material was very scarce, the ice hindered, and before the basement-story was fairly finished, winter had the pond under his lock and key.

In other localities I noticed that where the nests were placed on the banks of streams, they were made secure against the floods by being built amid a small clump of bushes. When the fall of 1879 came, the muskrats were very tardy about beginning their house, laying the cornerstone--or the corner-sod--about December 1, and continuing the work slowly and indifferently. On the 15th of the month the nest was not yet finished. "Maybe," I said, "this indicates a mild winter;" and, sure enough, the season was one of the mildest known for many years. The rats had little use for their house.

Again, in the fall of 1880, while the weather-wise were wagging their heads, some forecasting a mild, some a severe winter, I watched with interest for a sign from my muskrats. About November 1, a month earlier than the previous year, they began their nest, and worked at it with a will. They appeared to have just got tidings of what was coming. If I had taken the hint so palpably given, my celery would not have been frozen up in the ground, and my apples caught in unprotected places. When the cold wave struck us, about November 20, my four-legged "I told-you-so's" had nearly completed their dwelling; it lacked only the ridge-board, so to speak; it needed a little "topping out," to give it a finished look. But this it never got. The winter had come to stay, and it waxed more and more severe, till the unprecedented cold of the last days of December must have astonished even the wise muskrats in their snug retreat. I approached their nest at this time, a white mound upon the white, deeply frozen surface of the pond, and wondered if there was any life in that apparent sepulchre. I thrust my walking-stick sharply into it, when there was a rustle and a splash into the water, as the occupant made his escape. What a damp basement that house has, I thought, and what a pity to rout a peaceful neighbor out of his bed in this weather, and into such a state of things as this! But water does not wet the muskrat; his fur is charmed, and not a drop penetrates it.

Where the ground is favorable, the muskrats do not build these mound-like nests, but burrow into the bank a long distance, and establish their winter quarters there.

The muskrat does not hibernate like some rodents, but is pretty active all winter. In December I noticed in my walk where they had made excursions of a few yards to an orchard for frozen apples. One day, along a little stream, I saw a mink track amid those of the muskrat; following it up, I presently came to blood and other marks of strife upon the snow beside a stone wall. Looking in between the stones, I found the carcass of the luckless rat, with its head and neck eaten away. The mink had made a meal of him.

VI
THE SKUNK

In February a new track appears upon the snow, slender and delicate, about a third larger than that of the gray squirrel, indicating no haste or speed, but, on the contrary, denoting the most imperturbable ease and leisure, the footprints so close together that the trail appears like a chain of curiously carved links. Sir *Mephitis mephitica*, or, in plain English, the skunk, has waked up from his six weeks' nap, and come out into society again. He is a nocturnal traveler, very bold and impudent, coming quite up to the barn and outbuildings, and sometimes taking up his quarters for the season under the haymow. There is no such word as hurry in his dictionary, as you may see by his path upon the snow. He has a very sneaking, insinuating way, and goes creeping about the fields and woods, never once in a perceptible degree altering his gait, and, if a fence crosses his course, steers for a break or opening to avoid climbing. He is too indolent even to dig his own hole, but appropriates that of a woodchuck, or hunts out a crevice in the rocks, from which he extends his rambling in all directions, preferring damp, thawy weather. He has very little discretion or cunning, and holds a trap in utter contempt, stepping into it as soon as beside it, relying implicitly for defense against all forms of danger upon the unsavory punishment he is capable of inflicting. He is quite indifferent to both man and beast, and will not hurry himself to get out of the way of either. Walking through the summer fields at twilight, I have come near stepping upon him, and was much the more disturbed of the two.

He has a secret to keep and knows it, and is careful not to betray himself until he can do so with the most telling effect. I have known him to preserve his serenity even when caught in a steel trap, and look the very picture of injured innocence, manoeuvring carefully and deliberately to extricate his foot from the grasp of the naughty jaws. Do not by any means take pity on him, and lend a helping hand!

How pretty his face and head! How fine and delicate his teeth, like a weasel's or a cat's! When about a third grown, he looks so well that one covets him for a pet. My neighbor once captured a young one, which he kept over a year, and which afforded him much amusement. He named it Mahomet.

No animal is more cleanly in its habits than he. He is not an awkward boy who cuts his own face with his whip; and neither his flesh nor his fur hints the weapon with which he is armed. The most silent creature known to me, he makes no sound, so far as I have observed, save a diffuse, impatient noise, like that produced by beating your hand with a whisk-broom, when the farm-dog has discovered his retreat in the stone fence. He renders himself obnoxious to the farmer by his partiality for hens' eggs and young poultry. He is a confirmed epicure, and at plundering hen-roosts an expert. Not the full-grown fowls are his victims, but the youngest and most tender. At night Mother Hen receives under her maternal wings a dozen newly hatched chickens, and with much pride and satisfaction feels them all safely tucked away in her feathers. In the morning she is walking about disconsolately, attended by only two or three of all that pretty brood. What has happened? Where are they gone? That pickpocket, Sir Mephitis, could solve the mystery. Quietly has he approached, under cover of darkness, and one by one relieved her of her precious charge. Look closely, and you will see their little yellow legs and beaks, or part of a mangled form, lying about on the ground. Or, before the hen has hatched, he may find her out, and, by the same sleight of hand, remove every egg, leaving only the empty blood-stained shells to witness against him. The birds, especially the ground-builders, suffer in like manner from his plundering propensities.

The secretion upon which he relies for defense, and which is the chief source of his unpopularity, while it affords good reasons against cultivating him as a pet, and mars his attractiveness as game, is by no means the greatest indignity that can be offered to a nose. It is a rank, living smell, and has none of the sickening qualities of disease or putrefaction. Indeed, I think a good smeller will enjoy its most refined intensity. It approaches the sublime, and makes the nose tingle. It is tonic and bracing, and, I can readily believe, has rare medicinal qualities. I do not recommend its use as eye-water, though an old farmer assures me it has undoubted virtues when thus applied. Hearing, one night, a disturbance among his hens, he rushed suddenly out to catch the thief, when Sir Mephitis, taken by surprise, and no doubt much annoyed at being interrupted, discharged the vials of his wrath full in the farmer's face, and with such admirable effect that, for a few moments, he was completely blinded, and powerless to revenge himself upon the rogue, who embraced the opportunity to make good his escape; but he declared that afterwards his eyes felt as if purged by fire, and his sight was much clearer.

The skunk has perfect confidence in the efficacy of his weapon. Late one March afternoon in my walk, I saw one coming down through a field toward the highway. I thought I would intercept him and turn him back. I advanced to within fifteen or twenty yards of him, and, as he did not check his course, judged it prudent to check mine. On he came toward me, with the most jaunty and frolicsome air, waving his tail high above his head and challenging me to the combat. I retreated and he pursued, till I finally left him master of the field.

VII
THE FOX

It has been many a long day since I heard a fox bark, but in my youth among the Catskills I often heard the sound, especially of a still moonlight night in midwinter. Perhaps it was more a cry than a bark, not continuous like the baying of a dog, but uttered at intervals. One feels that the creature is trying to bark, but has not yet learned the trick of it. But it is a wild, weird sound. I would get up any night to hear it again. I used to listen for it when a boy, standing in front of my father's house. Presently I would hear one away up on the shoulder of the mountain, and I imagined I could almost see him sitting there in his furs upon the illuminated surface and looking down in my direction. As I listened, maybe one would answer him from behind the woods in the valley, a fitting sound amid the ghostly winter hills.

The red fox was the only species that abounded in this locality. On my way to school in the morning, after a fresh fall of snow, I would see at many points where he had crossed the road. Here he had leisurely passed within rifle-range of the house, evidently reconnoitring the premises with an eye to the hen-roost. That clear, sharp track,--there was no mistaking it for the clumsy footprint of a little dog. All his wildness and agility were photographed in it. Here he had taken fright, or suddenly recollected an engagement, and in long, graceful leaps, barely touching the fence, had gone careering up the hill as fleet as the wind.

The usual gait of the fox, unlike that of the dog, is, at night at least, a walk. On such occasions he is in quest of game and he goes through the woods and fields in an alert, stealthy manner, stepping about a foot at a time, and keeping his eyes and ears open.

The wild, buoyant creature, how beautiful he is! I had often seen his dead carcass, and at a distance had witnessed the hounds drive him across the upper fields; but the thrill and excitement of meeting him in his wild freedom in the woods were unknown to me till, one cold winter day, drawn thither by the baying of a hound, I stood near the summit of the mountain, waiting a renewal of the sound, that I might determine the course of the dog and choose my position,--stimulated by the ambition of all young Nimrods to bag some notable game. Long I waited, and patiently, till, chilled and benumbed, I was about to turn back, when, hearing a slight noise, I looked up and beheld a most superb fox, loping along with inimitable grace and ease, evidently disturbed, but not pursued by the hound, and so absorbed in his private meditations that he failed to see me, though I stood transfixed with amazement and admiration, not ten yards distant. I took his measure at a glance,--a large male, with dark legs, and massive tail tipped with white,--a most magnificent creature; but so astonished and fascinated was I by this sudden appearance and matchless beauty, that not till I had caught the last glimpse of him, as he disappeared over a knoll, did I awake to my duty as a sportsman, and realize what an opportunity to distinguish myself I had unconsciously let slip. I clutched my gun, half angrily, as if it was to blame, and went home out of humor with myself and all fox-kind. But I have since thought better of the experience, and concluded that I bagged the game after all, the best part of it, and fleeced Reynard of something more valuable than his fur, without his knowledge.

This is thoroughly a winter sound,--this voice of the hound upon the mountain,--and one that is music to many ears. The long trumpet-like bay, heard for a mile or more,--now faintly back to the deep recesses of the mountain,--now distinct, but still faint, as the hound comes over some prominent point and the wind favors,--anon entirely lost in the gully,--then breaking out again much nearer, and growing more and more pronounced as the dog approaches, till, when he comes around the brow of the mountain, directly above you, the barking is loud and sharp. On he goes along the northern spur, his voice rising and sinking as the wind and the lay of the ground modify it, till lost to hearing.

The fox usually keeps half a mile ahead, regulating his speed by that of the hound, occasionally pausing a moment to divert himself with a mouse, or to contemplate the landscape, or to listen for his pursuer. If the hound press him too closely, he leads off from mountain to mountain, and so generally escapes the hunter; but if the pursuit be slow, he plays about some ridge or peak, and falls a prey, though not an easy one, to the experienced sportsman.

A most spirited and exciting chase occurs when the farm-dog gets close upon one in the open field, as sometimes happens in the early morning. The fox relies so confidently upon his superior speed, that I imagine he half tempts the dog to the race. But if the dog be a smart one, and their course lies down hill, over smooth ground, Reynard must put his best foot forward, and then sometimes suffer the ignominy of being run over by his pursuer, who, however, is quite unable to pick him up, owing to the speed. But when they mount the hill, or enter the woods, the superior nimbleness and agility of the fox tell at once, and he easily leaves the dog far in his rear. For a cur less than his own size he manifests little fear, especially if the two meet alone, remote from the house. In such cases, I have seen first one turn tail, then the other.

One of the most notable features of the fox is his large and massive tail. Seen running on the snow at a distance, his tail is quite as conspicuous as his body; and, so far from appearing a burden, seems to contribute to his lightness and buoyancy. It softens the outline of his movements, and repeats or continues to the eye the ease and poise of his carriage. But, pursued by the hound on a wet, thawy day, it often becomes so heavy and bedraggled as to prove a serious inconvenience, and compels him to take refuge in his den. He is very loath to do this; both his pride and the traditions of his race stimulate him to run it out, and win by fair superiority of wind and speed; and only a wound or a heavy and moppish tail will drive him to avoid the issue in this manner.

To learn his surpassing shrewdness and cunning, attempt to take him with a trap. Rogue that he is, he always suspects some trick, and one must be more of a fox than he is himself to overreach him. At first sight it would appear easy enough. With apparent indifference he crosses your path, or walks in your footsteps in the field, or travels along the beaten highway, or lingers in the vicinity of stacks and remote barns. Carry the carcass of a pig, or a fowl, or a dog, to a distant field in mid-winter, and in a few nights his tracks cover the snow about it.

The inexperienced country youth, misled by this seeming carelessness of Reynard, suddenly conceives a project to enrich himself with fur, and wonders that the idea has not occurred to him before, and to others. I knew a youthful yeoman of this kind, who imagined he had found a mine of wealth on discovering on a remote side-hill, between two woods, a dead porker, upon which it appeared all the foxes of the neighborhood did nightly banquet. The clouds were burdened with snow; and as the first flakes commenced to eddy down, he set out, trap and broom in hand, already counting over in imagination the silver quarters he would receive for his first fox-skin. With the utmost care, and with a palpitating heart, he removed enough of the trodden snow to allow the trap to sink below the surface. Then, carefully sifting the light element over it and sweeping his tracks full, he quickly withdrew, laughing exultingly over the little surprise he had prepared for the cunning rogue. The elements conspired to aid him, and the falling snow rapidly obliterated all vestiges of his work. The next morning at dawn he was on his way to bring in his fur. The snow had done its work effectually, and, he believed, had kept his secret well. Arrived in sight of the locality, he strained his vision to make out his prize lodged against the fence at the foot of the hill. Approaching nearer, the surface was unbroken, and doubt usurped the place of certainty in his mind. A slight mound marked the site of the porker, but there was no footprint near it. Looking up the hill, he saw where Reynard had walked leisurely down toward his wonted bacon till within a few yards of it, when he had wheeled, and with prodigious strides disappeared in the woods. The young trapper saw at a glance what a comment this was upon his skill in the art, and, indignantly exhuming the iron, he walked home with it, the stream of silver quarters suddenly setting in another direction.

The successful trapper commences in the fall, or before the first deep snow. In a field not too remote, with an old axe he cuts a small place, say ten inches by fourteen, in the frozen ground, and removes the earth to the depth of three or four inches, then fills the cavity with dry ashes, in which are placed bits of roasted cheese. Reynard is very suspicious at first, and gives the place a wide berth. It looks like design, and he will see how the thing behaves before he approaches too near. But the cheese is savory and the cold severe. He ventures a little closer every night, until he can reach and pick a piece from the surface. Emboldened by success, like other mortals, he presently digs freely among the ashes, and, finding a fresh supply of the delectable morsels every night, is soon thrown off his guard and his suspicions quite lulled. After a week of baiting in this manner, and on the eve of a light fall of snow, the trapper carefully conceals his trap in the bed, first smoking it thoroughly with hemlock boughs to kill or neutralize all smell of the iron. If the weather favors and the proper precautions have been taken, he may succeed, though the chances are still greatly against him.

Reynard is usually caught very lightly, seldom more than the ends of his toes being between the jaws. He sometimes works so cautiously as to spring the trap without injury even to his toes, or may remove the cheese night after night without even springing it. I knew an old trapper who, on finding himself outwitted in this manner, tied a bit of cheese to the pan, and next morning had poor Reynard by the jaw. The trap is not fastened, but only incumbered with a clog, and is all the more sure in its hold by yielding to every effort of the animal to extricate himself.

When Reynard sees his captor approaching, he would fain drop into a mouse-hole to render himself invisible. He crouches to the ground and remains perfectly motionless until he perceives himself discovered, when he makes one desperate and final effort to escape, but ceases all struggling as you come up, and behaves in a manner that stamps him a very timid warrior,--cowering to the earth with a mingled look of shame, guilt, and humiliation. A young farmer told me of tracing one with his trap to the border of a wood, where he discovered the cunning rogue trying to hide by embracing a small tree. Most animals, when taken in a trap, show fight; but Reynard has more faith in the nimbleness of his feet than in the terror of his teeth.

I once spent a summer month in a mountainous district in the State of New York, where, from its earliest settlement, the red fox has been the standing prize for skill in the use of the trap and gun. At the house where I was stopping were two foxhounds, and a neighbor half a mile distant had a third. There were many others in the township, and in season they were well employed, too; but the three spoken of, attended by their owners, held high carnival on the mountains in the immediate vicinity. And many were the foxes that, winter after winter, fell before them, twenty-five having been shot, the season before my visit, on one small range alone. And yet the foxes were apparently never more abundant than they were that summer, and never bolder, coming at night within a few rods of the house and of the unchained alert hounds, and making havoc among the poultry.

One morning a large, fat goose was found minus her head and otherwise mangled. Both hounds had disappeared, and, as they did not come back till near night, it was inferred that they had cut short Reynard's repast, and given him a good chase into the bargain. But next night he was back again, and this time got safely off with the goose. A couple of nights after he must have come with recruits, for next morning three large goslings were reported missing. The silly geese now got it through their noddles that there was danger about, and every night thereafter came close up to the house to roost.

A brood of turkeys, the old one tied to a tree a few rods to the rear of the house, were the next objects of attack. The predaceous rascal came, as usual, in the latter half of the night. I happened to be awake, and heard the helpless turkey cry "Quit, quit," with great emphasis. Another sleeper, on the floor above me, who, it seems, had been sleeping with one ear awake for several nights in apprehension for the safety of his turkeys, heard the sound also, and instantly divined its cause. I heard the window open and a voice summon the dogs. A loud bellow was the response, which caused Reynard to take himself off in a hurry. A moment more, and the mother turkey would have shared the fate of the geese. There she lay at the end of her tether, with extended wings, bitten and rumpled. The young ones roosted in a row on the fence near by, and had taken flight on the first alarm.

Turkeys, retaining many of their wild instincts, are less easily captured by the fox than any other of our domestic fowls. On the slightest show of danger they take to wing, and it is not unusual, in the locality of which I speak, to find them in the morning perched in the most unwonted places, as on the peak of the barn or hay-shed, or on the tops of the apple-trees, their tails spread and their manners showing much excitement. Perchance one turkey is minus her tail, the fox having succeeded in getting only a mouthful of quills.

As the brood grows and their wings develop, they wander far from the house in quest of grasshoppers. At such times they are all watchfulness and suspicion. Crossing the fields one day, attended by a dog that much resembled a fox, I came suddenly upon a brood about one third grown, which were feeding in a pasture just beyond a wood. It so happened that they caught sight of the dog without seeing me, when instantly, with the celerity of wild game, they launched into the air, and, while the old one perched upon a treetop, as if to keep an eye on the supposed enemy, the young went sailing over the trees toward home.

The two hounds before referred to, accompanied by a cur-dog, whose business it was to mind the farm, but who took as much delight in running away from prosy duty as if he had been a schoolboy, would frequently steal off and have a good hunt all by themselves, just for the fun of the thing, I suppose. I more than half suspect that it was as a kind of taunt or retaliation that Reynard came and took the geese from under their very noses. One morning they went off and stayed till the afternoon of the next day; they ran the fox all day and all night, the hounds baying at every jump, the cur-dog silent and tenacious. When the trio returned they came dragging themselves along, stiff, foot-sore, gaunt, and hungry. For a day or two afterward they lay about the kennels, seeming to dread nothing so much as the having to move. The stolen hunt was their "spree," and of course they must take time to get over it.

Some old hunters think the fox enjoys the chase as much as the hound, especially when the latter runs slowly, as the best hounds do. The fox will wait for the hound, will sit down and listen, or play about, crossing and recrossing and doubling upon his track, as if enjoying a mischievous consciousness of the perplexity he would presently cause his pursuer. It is evident, however, that the fox does not always have his share of the fun: before a swift dog, or in a deep snow, or on a wet day when his tail gets heavy, he must put his best foot forward. As a last resort he "holes up." Sometimes he resorts to numerous devices to mislead and escape the dog altogether. He will walk in the bed of a small creek, or on a rail-fence. I heard of an instance of a fox, hard and long pressed, that took to a rail-fence, and, after walking some distance, made a leap to one side to a hollow stump, in the cavity of which he snugly stowed himself. The ruse succeeded, and the dogs lost the trail; but the hunter, coming up, passed by chance near the stump, when out bounded the fox, his cunning availing him less than he deserved. On another occasion the fox took to the public road, and stepped with great care and precision into a sleigh-track. The hard, polished snow took no imprint of the light foot, and the scent was no doubt less than it would have been on a rougher surface. Maybe, also, the rogue had considered the chances of another sleigh coming along, before the hound, and obliterating the trail entirely.

Audubon tells of a fox, which, when started by the hounds, always managed to elude them at a certain point. Finally the hunter concealed himself in the locality, to discover, if possible, the trick. Presently along came the fox, and, making a leap to one side, ran up the trunk of a fallen tree which had lodged some feet from the ground, and concealed himself in the top. In a few minutes the hounds came up, and in their eagerness passed some distance beyond the point, and then went still farther, looking for the lost trail. Then the fox hastened down, and, taking his back-track, fooled the dogs completely.

I was told of a silver-gray fox in northern New York, which, when pursued by the hounds, would run till it had hunted up another fox, or the fresh trail of one, when it would so manoeuvre that the hound would invariably be switched off on the second track.

In cold, dry weather the fox will sometimes elude the hound, at least delay him much, by taking to a bare, ploughed field. The hard, dry earth seems not to retain a particle of the scent, and the hound gives a loud, long, peculiar bark, to signify he has trouble. It is now his turn to show his wit, which he often does by passing completely around the field, and resuming the trail again where it crosses the fence or a strip of snow.

The fact that any dry, hard surface is unfavorable to the hound suggests, in a measure, the explanation of the wonderful faculty that all dogs in a degree possess of tracking an animal by the scent of the foot alone. Did you ever think why a dog's nose is always wet? Examine the nose of a fox-hound, for instance; how very moist and sensitive! Cause this moisture to dry up, and the dog would be as powerless to track an animal as you are! The nose of the cat, you may observe, is but a little moist, and, as you know, her sense of smell is far inferior to that of the dog. Moisten your own nostrils and lips, and this sense is plainly sharpened. The sweat of a dog's nose, therefore, is no doubt a vital element in its power, and, without taking a very long logical stride, we may infer how a damp, rough surface aids him in tracking game.

A still hunt rarely brings you in sight of a fox, as his ears are much sharper than yours, and his tread much lighter. But if the fox is mousing in the fields, and you discover him before he does you, you may, the wind favoring, call him within a few paces of you. Secrete yourself behind the fence, or some other object, and squeak as nearly like a mouse as possible. Reynard will hear the sound at an incredible distance. Pricking up his ears, he gets the direction, and comes trotting along as unsuspiciously as can be. I have never had an opportunity to try the experiment, but I know perfectly reliable persons who have. One man, in the pasture getting his cows, called a fox which was too busy mousing to get the first sight, till it jumped upon the wall just over where he sat secreted. He then sprang up, giving a loud whoop at the same time, and the fox, I suspect, came as near being frightened out of his skin as a fox ever was.

I have never been able to see clearly why the mother fox generally selects a burrow or hole in the open field in which to have her young, except it be, as some hunters maintain, for better security. The young foxes are wont to come out on a warm day, and play like puppies in front of the den. The view being unobstructed on all sides by trees or bushes, in the cover of which danger might approach, they are less liable to surprise and capture. On the slightest sound they disappear in the hole. Those who have watched the gambols of the young foxes speak of them as very amusing, even more arch and playful than those of kittens, while a spirit profoundly wise and cunning seems to look out of their young eyes. The parent fox can never be caught in the den with them, but is hovering near the woods, which are always at hand, and by her warning cry or bark telling them when to be on their guard. She usually has at least three dens, at no great distance apart, and moves stealthily in the night with her charge from one to the other, so as to mislead her enemies. Many a party of boys, and of men, too, discovering the whereabouts of a litter, have gone with shovels and picks, and, after digging away vigorously for several hours, have found only an empty hole for their pains. The old fox, finding her secret had been found out, had waited for darkness, in the cover of which to transfer her household to new quarters; or else some old fox-hunter, jealous of the preservation of his game, and getting word of the intended destruction of the litter, had gone at dusk the night before, and made some disturbance about the den, perhaps flashed some powder in its mouth,--a hint which the shrewd animal knew how to interpret.

The fox nearly always takes his nap during the day in the open fields, along the sides of the ridges, or under the mountain, where he can look down upon the busy farms beneath and hear their many sounds, the barking of dogs, the lowing of cattle, the cackling of hens, the voices of men and boys, or the sound of travel upon the highway. It is on that side, too, that he keeps the sharpest lookout, and the appearance of the hunter above and behind him is always a surprise.

Foxes, unlike wolves, never go in packs or companies, but hunt singly. Many of the ways and manners of the fox, when tamed, are like the dog's. I once saw a young red fox exposed for sale in the market in Washington. A colored man had him, and said he had caught him out in Virginia. He led him by a small chain, as he would a puppy, and the innocent young rascal would lie on his side and bask and sleep in the sunshine, amid all the noise and chaffering around him, precisely like a dog. He was about the size of a full-grown cat, and there was a bewitching beauty about him that I could hardly resist. On another occasion, I saw a gray fox, about two thirds grown, playing with a dog, about the same size, and by nothing in the manners of either could you tell which was the dog and which was the fox.

VIII
THE WEASEL

My most interesting note of the season of 1893 relates to a weasel. One day in early November, my boy and I were sitting on a rock at the edge of a tamarack swamp in the woods, hoping to get a glimpse of some grouse which we knew were in the habit of feeding in the swamp. We had not sat there very long before we heard a slight rustling in the leaves below us, which we at once fancied was made by the cautious tread of a grouse. (We had no gun.) Presently, through the thick brushy growth, we caught sight of a small animal running along, that we at first took for a red squirrel. A moment more, and it came into full view but a few yards from us, and we saw that it was a weasel. A second glance showed that it carried something in its mouth which, as it drew near, we saw was a mouse or a mole of some sort. The weasel ran nimbly along, now the length of a decayed log, then over stones and branches, pausing a moment every three or four yards, and passed within twenty feet of us, and disappeared behind some rocks on the bank at the edge of the swamp. "He is carrying food into his den," I said; "let us watch him." In four or five minutes he reappeared, coming back over the course along which he had just passed, running over and under the same stones and down the same decayed log, and was soon out of sight in the swamp. We had not moved, and evidently he had not noticed us. After about six minutes we heard the same rustle as at first, and in a moment saw the weasel coming back with another mouse in his mouth. He kept to his former route as if chained to it, making the same pauses and gestures, and repeating exactly his former movements. He disappeared on our left as before, and, after a few moments' delay, reemerged and took his course down into the swamp again. We waited about the same length of time as before, when back he came with another mouse. He evidently had a big crop of mice down there amid the bogs and bushes, and he was gathering his harvest in very industriously. We became curious to see exactly where his den was, and so walked around where he had seemed to disappear each time, and waited. He was as punctual as usual, and was back with his game exactly on time. It happened that we had stopped within two paces of his hole, so that, as he approached it, he evidently discovered us. He paused, looked steadily at us, and then, without any sign of fear, entered his den. The entrance was not under the rocks as we had expected to find it, but was in the bank a few feet beyond them. We remained motionless for some time, but he did not reappear. Our presence had made him suspicious, and he was going to wait a while. Then I removed some dry leaves and exposed his doorway, a small, round hole, hardly as large as the chipmunk makes, going straight down into the ground. We had a lively curiosity to get a peep into his larder. If he had been carrying in mice at this rate very long, his cellars must be packed with them. With a sharp stick I began digging into the red clayey soil, but soon encountered so many roots from near trees that I gave it up, deciding to return next day with a mattock. So I repaired the damages I had done as well as I could, replacing the leaves, and we moved off.

The next day, which was mild and still, I came back prepared, as I thought, to unearth the weasel and his treasures. I sat down where we had sat the day before and awaited developments. I was curious to know if the weasel was still carrying in his harvest. I had sat but a few minutes when I heard again the rustle in the dry leaves, and saw the weasel coming home with another mouse. I observed him till he had made three trips; about every six or seven minutes, I calculated, he brought in a mouse. Then I went and stood near his hole. This time he had a fat meadow-mouse. He laid it down near the entrance, went in and turned around, and reached out and drew the mouse in after him. That store of mice I am bound to see, I thought, and then fell to with the heavy mattock. I followed the hole down about two feet, when it turned to the north. I kept the clue by thrusting into the passage slender twigs; these it was easy to follow. Two or three feet more and the hole branched, one part going west, the other northeast. I followed the west one a few feet till it branched. Then I turned to the easterly tunnel, and pursued it till it branched. I followed one of these ways till it divided. I began to be embarrassed and hindered by the accumulations of loose soil. Evidently this weasel had foreseen just such an assault upon his castle as I was making, and had planned it accordingly. He was not to be caught napping. I found several enlargements in the various tunnels, breathing spaces, or spaces to turn around in, or to meet and chat with a companion, but nothing that looked like a terminus, a permanent living-room. I tried removing the soil a couple of paces away with the mattock, but found it slow work. I was getting warm and tired, and my task was apparently only just begun. The farther I dug, the more numerous and intricate became the passages. I concluded to stop, and come again the next day, armed with a shovel in addition to the mattock.

Accordingly, I came back on the morrow, and fell to work vigorously. I soon had quite a large excavation; I found the bank a labyrinth of passages, with here and there a large chamber. One of the latter I struck only six inches under the surface, by making a fresh breach a few feet away.

While I was leaning upon my shovel-handle and recovering my breath, I heard some light-footed creature tripping over the leaves above me just out of view, which I fancied might be a squirrel. Presently I heard the bay of a hound and the yelp of a cur, and then knew that a rabbit had passed near me. The dogs came hurrying after, with a great rumpus, and then presently the hunters followed. The dogs remained barking not many rods south of me on the edge of the swamp, and I knew the rabbit had run to hole. For half an hour or more I heard the hunters at work there, digging their game out; then they came along and discovered me at my work. They proved to be an old trapper and woodsman and his son. I told them what I was in quest of. "A mountain weasel," said the old man. "Seven or eight years ago I used to set deadfalls for rabbits just over there, and the game was always partly eaten up. It must have been this weasel that visited my traps." So my game was evidently an old resident of the place. This swamp, maybe, had been his hunting-ground for many years, and he had added another hall to his dwelling each year. After further digging, I struck at least one of his banqueting halls, a cavity about the size of one's hat, arched over by a network of fine tree-roots. The occupant evidently lodged or rested here also. There was a warm, dry nest, made of leaves and the fur of mice and moles. I took out two or three handfuls. In finding this chamber I had followed one of the tunnels around till it brought me within a foot of the original entrance. A few inches to one side of this cavity there was what I took to be a back alley where the weasel threw his waste; there were large masses of wet, decaying fur here, and fur pellets such as are regurgitated by hawks and owls. In the nest there was the tail of a flying squirrel, showing that the weasel sometimes had this game for supper or dinner.

I continued my digging with renewed energy; I should yet find the grand depot where all these passages centred; but the farther I excavated, the more complex and baffling the problem became; the ground was honeycombed with passages. What enemy has this weasel, I said to myself, that he should provide so many ways of escape, that he should have a back door at every turn? To corner him would be impossible; to be lost in his fortress was like being lost in Mammoth Cave. How he could bewilder his pursuer by appearing now at this door, now at that; now mocking him from the attic, now defying him from the cellar! So far, I had discovered but one entrance; but some of the chambers were so near the surface that it looked as if the planner had calculated upon an emergency when he might want to reach daylight quickly in a new place.

Finally I paused, rested upon my shovel a while, eased my aching back upon the ground, and then gave it up, feeling as I never had before the force of the old saying, that you cannot catch a weasel asleep. I had made an ugly hole in the bank, had handled over two or three times a ton or more of earth, and was apparently no nearer the weasel and his store of mice than when I began.

Then I regretted that I had broken into his castle at all; that I had not contented myself with coming day after day and counting his mice as he carried them in, and continued my observation upon him each succeeding year. Now the rent in his fortress could not be repaired, and he would doubtless move away, as he most certainly did, for his doors, which I had closed with soil, remained unopened after winter had set in.

But little seems known about the intimate private lives of any of our lesser wild creatures. It was news to me that any of the weasels lived in dens in this way, and that they stored up provision against a day of need. This species was probably the little ermine, eight or nine inches long, with tail about five inches. It was still in its summer dress of dark chestnut-brown above and whitish below.

It was a mystery where the creature had put the earth which it must have removed in digging its den; not a grain was to be seen anywhere, and yet a bushel or more must have been taken out. Externally, there was not the slightest sign of that curious habitation there under the ground. The entrance was hidden beneath dry leaves, and was surrounded by little passages and flourishes between the leaves and the ground. If any of my readers find a weasel's den, I hope they will be wiser than I was, and observe his goings and comings without disturbing his habitation.

A few years later I had another adventure with a weasel that had its den in a bank on the margin of a muck swamp in the same neighborhood. We had cleared and drained and redeemed the swamp and made it into a garden, and I had built me a lodge there. The weasel's hunting-grounds, where doubtless he had been wont to gather his supply of mice, had been destroyed, and he had "got even" with me by preying upon my young chickens. Night after night the number of chickens grew less, till one day we chanced to see the creature boldly chasing one of the larger fowls along the road near the henhouse. His career was cut short then and there by one of the men. We were then ignorant of the den in the bank a few yards away. The next season my chickens were preyed upon again; they were killed upon the roost, and their half-eaten bodies were found under the floor. One night I was awakened about midnight by that loud, desperate cry which a barn fowl gives when suddenly seized upon its roost. Was I dreaming, or was that a cry of murder from my chickens? I seized my lantern, and with my dog rushed out to where a pair of nearly grown roosters passed the nights upon a low stump. They were both gone, and the action of the dog betrayed the fresh scent of some animal. But we could get no clue to the chickens or their enemy. I felt sure that only one of the fowls had been seized, and that the other had dashed away wildly in the darkness, which proved to be the case. The dead chicken was there under the edge of the stump, where I found it in the morning, and its companion came forth unhurt during the day. Thenceforth the chickens, big and little, were all shut up in the henhouse at night. On the third day the appetite of the weasel was keen again, and it boldly gave chase to a chicken before our eyes. I was standing in my porch with my dog, talking with my neighbor and his wife, who, with their dog, were standing in the road a few yards in front of me. A chicken suddenly screamed in the bushes up behind the rocks just beyond my friends. Then it came rushing down over the rocks past them, flying and screaming, closely pursued by a long, slim red animal, that seemed to slide over the rocks like a serpent. Its legs were so short that one saw only the swift, gliding motion of its body. Across the road into the garden, within a yard of my friends, went the pursued and the pursuer, and into the garden rushed I and my dog. The weasel seized the chicken by the wing, and was being dragged along by the latter in its effort to escape, when I arrived upon the scene. With a savage glee I had not felt for many a day, I planted my foot upon the weasel. The soft muck underneath yielded, and I held him without hurting him. He let go his hold upon the chicken and seized the sole of my shoe in his teeth. Then I reached down and gripped him with my thumb and forefinger just back of the ears, and lifted him up, and looked his impotent rage in the face. What gleaming eyes, what an array of threatening teeth, what reaching of vicious claws, what a wriggling and convulsed body! But I held him firmly. He could only scratch my hand and dart fire from his electric, bead-like eyes. In the mean time my dog was bounding up, begging to be allowed to have his way with the weasel. But I knew what he did not: I knew that in anything like a fair encounter the weasel would get the first hold, would draw the first blood, and hence probably effect his escape. So I carried the animal, writhing and scratching, to a place in the road removed from any near cover, and threw him violently upon the ground, hoping thereby so to stun and bewilder him that the terrier could rush in and crush him before he recovered his wits. But I had miscalculated; the blow did indeed stun and confuse him, but he was still too quick for the dog, and had him by the lip like an electric trap. Nip lifted up his head and swung the weasel violently about in the air, trying to shake him off, uttering a cry of rage and pain, but did not succeed in loosening the animal's hold for some moments. When he had done so, and attempted to seize him a second time, the weasel was first again, but quickly released his hold and darted about this way and that, seeking cover. Three or four times the dog was upon him, but found him each time too hot to be held. Seeing that the creature was likely to escape, I set my foot upon him again, and made a finish of him.

The weasel is the boldest and most bloodthirsty of our small mammals; indeed, none of our larger beasts are more so. There is something devilish and uncanny about it. It persists like fate; it eludes, but cannot be eluded. The terror it inspires in the smaller creatures--rats, rabbits, chipmunks--is pitiful to behold. A rat pursued by a weasel has been known to rush into a room, uttering dismal cries, and seek the protection of a man in bed. A chipmunk will climb to the top of a tall tree to elude it, and then, when followed, let go its hold and drop with a cry of despair toward the ground. A friend of mine, walking along the road early one morning, saw a rat rush over the fence and cross a few yards ahead of him. Pressing it close came a weasel, which seized the rat before it could gain the opposite wall. My friend rushed to the aid of the rat with his cane. But the weasel dodged his blows, and in a moment or two turned fiercely upon him. My friend aimed more blows at it without effect, when the weasel began leaping up before him, within a few feet of his face, its eyes gleaming, its teeth threatening, and dodging every blow aimed at it. The effect, my friend says, was singularly uncanny and startling. It was like some infuriated imp of Satan dancing before him, and watching for a chance to seize him by the throat or to dash into his eyes. He slowly backed off, beating the air with his cane. Then the weasel returned to the disabled rat and attempted to drag it into the wall. My friend now began to hurl stones at it, but it easily dodged them. Now he was joined by another passer-by, and the two opened upon the weasel with stones, till finally, in dodging one, it was caught by the other, and so much hurt that it gave up the rat and sought shelter in the wall, where it was left waiting to secure its game when its enemies should have gone on.

I must give one more instance of the boldness and ferocity of the weasel. A woman in northern Vermont discovered that something was killing her hens, often on the nest. She watched for the culprit, and at last caught a weasel in the act. It had seized the hen, and refused to let go when she tried to scare it away. Then the woman laid hold of it and tried choking it, when the weasel released its hold upon the hen and fastened its teeth into her hand between the thumb and forefinger. She could not choke it off, and ran to a neighbor for help, but no one could remove it without tearing the flesh from the woman's hand. Then some one suggested a pail of water; into this the hand and weasel were plunged, but the creature would not let go even then, and did not until it was drowned.

The weasel is a subtle and destructive enemy of the birds. It climbs trees and explores them with great ease and nimbleness. I have seen it do so on several occasions. One day my attention was arrested by the angry notes of a pair of brown thrashers that were flitting from bush to bush along an old stone wall in a remote field. Presently I saw what it was that excited them,--three large red weasels, or ermines, coming along the stone wall, and leisurely and half playfully exploring every tree that stood near it. They had probably robbed the thrashers. They would go up the trees with great ease, and glide serpent-like out upon the main branches. When they descended the tree, they were unable to come straight down, like a squirrel, but went around it spirally. How boldly they thrust their heads out of the wall, and eyed me and sniffed me as I drew near,--their round, thin ears, their prominent, glistening, bead-like eyes, and the curving, snake-like motions of the head and neck being very noticeable. They looked like blood-suckers and egg-suckers. They suggested something extremely remorseless and cruel. One could understand the alarm of the rats when they discover one of these fearless, subtle, and circumventing creatures threading their holes. To flee must be like trying to escape death itself. I was one day standing in the woods upon a flat stone, in what at certain seasons was the bed of a stream, when one of these weasels came undulating along and ran under the stone upon which I was standing. As I remained motionless, he thrust out his wedge-shaped head, and turned it back above the stone as if half in mind to seize my foot; then he drew back, and presently went his way. These weasels often hunt in packs like the British stoat. When I was a boy, my father one day armed me with an old musket and sent me to shoot chipmunks around the corn. While watching the squirrels, a troop of weasels tried to cross a bar-way where I sat, and were so bent on doing it that I fired at them, boy-like, simply to thwart their purpose. One of the weasels was disabled by my shot, but the troop was not discouraged, and, after making several feints to cross, one of them seized the wounded one and bore it over, and the pack disappeared in the wall on the other side.

Let me conclude this chapter with two or three more notes about this alert enemy of the birds and lesser animals, the weasel.

A farmer one day heard a queer growling sound in the grass: on approaching the spot he saw two weasels contending over a mouse; both held the mouse, pulling in opposite directions, and they were so absorbed in the struggle that the farmer cautiously put his hands down and grabbed them both by the back of the neck. He put them in a cage, and offered them bread and other food. This they refused to eat, but in a few days one of them had eaten the other up, picking his bones clean, and leaving nothing but the skeleton.

The same farmer was one day in his cellar when two rats came out of a hole near him in great haste, and ran up the cellar wall and along its top till they came to a floor timber that stopped their progress, when they turned at bay, and looked excitedly back along the course they had come. In a moment a weasel, evidently in hot pursuit of them, came out of the hole, but, seeing the farmer, checked his course and darted back. The rats had doubtless turned to give him fight, and would probably have been a match for him.

The weasel seems to track its game by scent. A hunter of my acquaintance was one day sitting in the woods, when he saw a red squirrel run with great speed up a tree near him, and out upon a long branch, from which he leaped to some rocks, disappearing beneath them. In a moment a weasel came in full course upon his trail, ran up the tree, then out along the branch, leaping from there to the rocks just as the squirrel had done and pursuing him into their recesses.

Doubtless the squirrel fell a prey to him. The squirrel's best game would have been to keep to the higher treetops, where he could easily have distanced the weasel. But beneath the rocks he stood a very poor chance. I have often wondered what keeps such an animal as the weasel in check, for they are quite rare. They never need go hungry, for rats and squirrels and mice and birds are everywhere. They probably do not fall a prey to any other animal, and they are very rarely captured or killed by man. But the circumstances or agencies that check the increase of any species of animal are, as Darwin says, very obscure and but little known.

IX
THE MINK

In walking through the woods one day in early winter, we read upon the newly fallen snow the record of a mink's fright the night before. The mink had been traveling through the woods post-haste, not along the watercourses where one sees them by day, but over ridges and across valleys. We followed his track some distance to see what adventures he had met with. We tracked him through a bushy swamp, and saw where he had left it to explore a pile of rocks, then where he had taken to the swamp again, and where he had entered the more open woods. Presently the track turned sharply about, and doubled upon itself in long hurried strides. What had caused the mink to change his mind so suddenly? We explored a few paces ahead, and came upon a fox track. The mink had probably seen the fox stalking stealthily through the woods, and the sight had doubtless brought his heart into his mouth. I think he climbed a tree, and waited till the fox had passed. His track disappeared amid a clump of hemlocks, and then reappeared again a little beyond them. It described a big loop around, and then crossed the fox track only a few yards from the point where its course was interrupted. Then it followed a little watercourse, went under a rude bridge in a wood-road, then mingled with squirrel tracks in a denser part of the thicket. If the mink met a muskrat or a rabbit in his travels, or came upon a grouse, or quail, or a farmer's henroost, he had the supper he was in quest of.

I followed a mink's track one morning upon the snow till I found where the prowler had overtaken and killed a muskrat by a stone wall near a little stream. The blood upon the snow and the half-devoured body of the rat told the whole story. The mink is very fond of muskrats, and trappers often use this flesh to bait their traps. I wonder if he has learned to enter the under-water hole to the muskrat's den, and then seek him in his chamber above, where the poor rat would have little chance to escape.

The mink is only a larger weasel, and has much of the boldness and blood-thirstiness of that animal. One summer day my dog Lark and I were sitting beside a small watercourse in the woods, when I saw a mink coming up the stream toward us. I sat motionless till the mink was within a few feet of us, when the dog saw him. As the dog sprang, the mink darted under a large flat stone. Lark was very fierce, and seemed to say to me, "Just lift up that stone and I will show you my way with minks." This I quickly did, and the dog sprang for the game, but he as quickly withdrew with a cry of pain as if he had touched something red-hot. The mink had got in the first blow or bite, and then effected his escape between my feet and the dog's, as if he had vanished in the air. Where he went to was a mystery. There was no hole; no depth of water; no hiding-place anywhere that I could discover or that the dog could discover, and yet the mink had disappeared. It was like some conjurer's trick.

Minks are fond of fish, and can capture them in the water. This makes them very destructive along small trout streams and ponds. I once saw a trout with an ugly gash in its side, which was doubtless the work of a mink. With a friend, I once had a camp by a trout stream in the Catskills that we named "Mink Camp," by reason of the number of minks that came every night as soon as it was dark, to devour the fish-heads and entrails that we threw over on the opposite bank. We could often hear them disputing over the spoils, and in the dim light of the camp-fire could sometimes see them.

You may know the mink's track upon the snow from those of the squirrels at once. In the squirrel-track the prints of the large hind feet are ahead, with the prints of the smaller fore feet just behind them, as in the case of the rabbit. The mink, in running, usually plants his hind feet exactly upon the track of his fore feet, and closer together than the squirrel, so that his trail upon the snow is something like this:--

The squirrel's track, as well as those of the rabbit and the white-footed mouse, is in form like this:--

One winter day I had a good view of a mink running upon the snow and ice along the edge of a stream. He had seen or heard me, and was making a little extra speed. He bounded along with his back much arched, in a curiously stiff and mechanical sort of way, with none of the grace and ease of the squirrel. He leaped high, and cleared about two and a half feet at a bound.

X
THE RACCOON

In March that brief summary of a bear, the raccoon, comes out of his den in the ledges, and leaves his sharp digitigrade track upon the snow,--traveling not unfrequently in pairs,--a lean, hungry couple, bent on pillage and plunder. They have an unenviable time of it,--feasting in the summer and fall, hibernating in winter, and starving in spring. In April I have found the young of the previous year creeping about the fields, so reduced by starvation as to be quite helpless, and offering no resistance to my taking them up by the tail and carrying them home. The old ones also become very much emaciated, and come boldly up to the barn or other out-buildings in quest of food. I remember, one morning in early spring, hearing old Cuff, the farm-dog, barking vociferously before it was yet light. When we got up we discovered him at the foot of an ash-tree, which stood about thirty rods from the house, looking up at some gray object in the leafless branches, and by his manners and his voice evincing great impatience that we were so tardy in coming to his assistance. Arrived on the spot, we saw in the tree a coon of unusual size. One bold climber proposed to go up and shake it down. This was what old Cuff wanted, and he fairly bounded with delight as he saw his young master shinning up the tree. Approaching within eight or ten feet of the coon, the climber seized the branch to which it clung and shook long and fiercely. But the coon was in no danger of losing its hold; and when the climber paused to renew his hold it turned toward him with a growl, and showed very clearly a purpose to advance to the attack. This caused its pursuer to descend to the ground again with all speed. When the coon was finally brought down with a gun, it fought the dog, which was a large, powerful animal, with great fury, returning bite for bite for some moments; and after a quarter of an hour had elapsed, and its unequal antagonist had shaken it as a terrier does a rat, making his teeth meet through the small of its back, the coon still showed fight.

The coon is very tenacious of life, and like the badger will always whip a dog of its own size and weight. A woodchuck can bite severely, having teeth that cut like chisels, but a coon has agility and power of limb as well.

Coons are considered game only in the fall, or towards the close of summer, when they become fat and their flesh sweet. At this time, cooning is a famous pastime in the remote interior. As these animals are entirely nocturnal in their habits, they are hunted only at night. A piece of corn on some remote side-hill near the mountain, or between two pieces of woods, is most apt to be frequented by them. While the corn is yet green they pull the ears down like hogs, and, tearing open the sheathing of husks, eat the tender, succulent kernels, bruising and destroying much more than they devour. Sometimes their ravages are a matter of serious concern to the farmer. But every such neighborhood has its coon-dog, and the boys and young men dearly love the sport. The party sets out about eight or nine o'clock of a dark, moonless night, and stealthily approaches the cornfield. The dog knows his business, and when he is put into a patch of corn and told to "hunt them up" he makes a thorough search, and will not be misled by any other scent. You hear him rattling through the corn, hither and yon, with great speed. The coons prick up their ears, and quickly take themselves off on the opposite side of the field. In the stillness you may sometimes hear a single stone rattle on the wall as they hurry toward the woods. If the dog finds nothing he comes back to his master in a short time, and says in his dumb way, "No coon there." But if he strikes a trail you presently hear a louder rattling on the stone wall, and then a hurried bark as he enters the woods, succeeded in a few minutes by loud and repeated barkings as he reaches the foot of the tree in which the coon has taken refuge. Then follows a pellmell rush as the cooning party dash up the hill, into the woods, through the brush and the darkness, falling over prostrate trees, pitching into gullies and hollows, losing hats and tearing clothes, till finally, guided by the baying of the faithful dog, they reach the tree. The first thing now in order is to kindle a fire, and, if its light reveals the coon, to shoot him; if not, to fell the tree with an axe, unless this last expedient happens to be too great a sacrifice of timber and of strength, in which case it is necessary to sit down at the foot of the tree and wait till morning.

XI
THE PORCUPINE

Among our wild animals there are three that are slow-moving, dull-witted, and almost fearless,--the skunk, the opossum, and the porcupine. The two latter seem to be increasing in most parts of the country. The opossum is becoming quite common in the valley of the Hudson, and the porcupine is frequently met with in parts of the country where it was rarely or never seen forty years ago.

When the boys in late fall now go cooning where I used to go cooning in my youth, the dogs often run on a porcupine or drive him up a tree, and thus the sport is interrupted. Sometimes the dog comes to them with his mouth stuck full of quills, and is then compelled to submit to the painful operation of having them withdrawn. A sportsman relates that he once came upon a dead porcupine and a dead bald eagle lying upon the ground within a few yards of each other. The eagle had partly torn the porcupine to pieces, but in attacking it with its beak it had driven numerous spines of the animal into its throat, and from their effect had apparently died as soon as its victim.

The quill of a porcupine is like a bad habit: if it once gets hold it constantly works deeper and deeper, though the quill has no power of motion in itself; it is the live, active flesh of its victim that draws it in by means of the barbed point. One day my boy and I encountered a porcupine on the top of one of the Catskills, and we had a little circus with him; we wanted to wake him up, and make him show a little excitement, if possible. Without violence or injury to him, we succeeded to the extent of making his eyes fairly stand out from his head, but quicken his motion he would not,--probably could not.

What astonished and alarmed him seemed to be that his quills had no effect upon his enemies; they laughed at his weapons. He stuck his head under a rock and left his back and tail exposed. This is the porcupine's favorite position of defense. "Now come if you dare," he seems to say. Touch his tail, and like a trap it springs up and strikes your hand full of little quills. The tail is the active weapon of defense; with this the animal strikes. It is the outpost that delivers its fire before the citadel is reached. It is doubtless this fact that has given rise to the popular notion that the porcupine can shoot its quills, which of course it cannot do.

With a rotten stick we sprang the animal's tail again and again, till its supply of quills began to run low, and the creature grew uneasy. "What does this mean?" he seemed to say, his excitement rising. His shield upon his back, too, we trifled with, and when we finally drew him forth with a forked stick, his eyes were ready to burst from his head. In what a peevish, injured tone the creature did complain of our unfair tactics! He protested and protested, and whimpered and scolded, like some infirm old man tormented by boys. His game after we led him forth was to keep himself as much as possible in the shape of a ball, but with two sticks and a cord we finally threw him over on his back and exposed his quill-less and vulnerable under side, when he fairly surrendered and seemed to say, "Now you may do with me as you like." Then we laughed in his face and went our way.

Before we had reached our camp I was suddenly seized with a strange, acute pain in one of my feet. It seemed as if a large nerve was being roughly sawed in two. I could not take another step. Sitting down and removing my shoe and stocking, I searched for the cause of the paralyzing pain. The foot was free from mark or injury, but what was that little thorn or fang of thistle doing on the ankle? I pulled it out and found it to be one of the lesser quills of the porcupine. By some means, during our "circus," the quill had dropped inside my stocking, the thing had "taken," and the porcupine had his revenge for all the indignities we had put upon him. I was well punished. The nerve which the quill struck had unpleasant memories of it for many months afterward. When you come suddenly upon the porcupine in his native haunts, he draws his head back and down, puts up his shield, trails his broad tail, and waddles slowly away. His shield is the sheaf of larger quills upon his back, which he opens and spreads out in a circular form so that the whole body is quite hidden beneath it. The porcupine's great chisel-like teeth, which are quite as formidable as those of the woodchuck, he does not appear to use at all in his defense, but relies entirely upon his quills, and when those fail him he is done for.

I once passed a summer night alone upon the highest peak of the Catskills, Slide Mountain. I soon found there were numerous porcupines that desired to keep me company. The news of my arrival in the afternoon seemed to have spread rapidly among them. They probably had scented me. After resting awhile I set out to look up the spring, and met a porcupine on his way toward my camp. He turned out in the grass, and then, as I paused, came back into the path and passed directly over my feet. He evidently felt that he had as good a right to the road as I had; he had traveled it many times before me. When I charged upon him with a stick in my hand, he slowly climbed a small balsam fir.

I soon found the place of the spring, and, having dredged it and cleaned it, I sat down upon a rock and waited for the water slowly to seep in. Presently I heard something in the near bushes, and in a moment a large porcupine came into view. I thought that he, too, was looking for water; but no, he was evidently on his way to my camp. He, also, had heard the latest rumor on the mountain-top. It was highly amusing to watch his movements. He came teetering along in the most aimless, idiotic way. Now he drifted off a little to the right, then a little to the left; his blunt nose seemed vaguely to be feeling the air; he fumbled over the ground, tossed about by loose boulders and little hillocks; his eyes wandered stupidly about; I was in plain view within four or five yards of him, but he heeded me not. Then he turned back a few paces, but some slight obstacle in his way caused him to change his mind. One thought of a sleep-walker; uncertainty was stamped upon every gesture and movement; yet he was really drifting towards camp. After a while he struck the well-defined trail, and his gray, shapeless body slowly disappeared up the slope. In five or six minutes I overtook him shuffling along within sight of the big rock upon which rested my blanket and lunch. As I came up to him he depressed his tail, put up his shield, and slowly pushed off into the wild grass. While I was at lunch I heard a sound, and there he was, looking up at me from the path a few feet away. "An uninvited guest," I said; "but come on." He hesitated, and then turned aside into the bracken; he would wait till I had finished and had gone to sleep, or had moved off.

How much less wit have such animals,--animals like the porcupine, opossum, skunk, turtle,--that nature has armed against all foes, than the animals that have no such ready-made defenses, and are preyed upon by a multitude of enemies! The price paid for being shielded against all danger, for never feeling fear or anxiety, is stupidity. If the porcupine were as vulnerable to its enemies as, say, the woodchuck, it would probably soon come to be as alert and swift of foot as that marmot.

For an hour or more, that afternoon on the mountain top, my attention was attracted by a peculiar continuous sound that seemed to come from far away to the east. I queried with myself, "Is it the sound of some workman in a distant valley hidden by the mountains, or is its source nearer by me on the mountain side?" I could not determine. It was not a hammering or a grating or the filing of a saw, though it suggested such sounds. It had a vague, distant, ventriloquial character. In the solitude of the mountain top there was something welcome and pleasing in it. Finally I set out to try to solve the mystery. I had not gone fifty yards from camp when I knew I was near the source of the sound. Presently I saw a porcupine on a log, and as I approached the sound ceased, and the animal moved away. A curious kind of chant he made, or note of wonder and surprise at my presence on the mountain,--or was he calling together the clan for a midnight raid upon my camp?

I made my bed that night of ferns and balsam boughs under an overhanging rock, where the storm that swept across the mountain just after dark could not reach me. I lay down, rolled in my blankets, with a long staff by my side, in anticipation of visits from the porcupines. In the middle of the night I was awakened, and, looking out of my den, saw a porcupine outlined against the starlit sky. I made a thrust at him with my staff, when, with a grunt or grumble, he disappeared. A little later I was awakened again by the same animal, or another, which I repelled as before. At intervals during the rest of the night they visited me in this way; my sleep was by short stages from one porcupine to another.

These animals are great gnawers. They seem to be specially fond of gnawing any tool or object that has been touched or used by human hands. They would probably have gnawed my shoes or lunch basket or staff had I lain still. A settler at the foot of the mountain told me they used to prove very annoying to him by getting into his cellar or woodshed at night, and indulging their ruling passion by chewing upon his tool-handles or pails or harness. "Kick one of them outdoors," he said, "and in half an hour he is back again." In winter they usually live in trees, gnawing the bark and feeding upon the inner layer. I have seen large hemlocks quite denuded and killed in this way.

XII
THE OPOSSUM

A new track has appeared upon the snow in my neighborhood here on the Hudson within the past few years. It is a strange track, and suggests some small, deformed human hand. If the dwarfs or brownies we read of in childhood were to walk abroad in winter, they might leave such an imprint behind them as this.

This track, which we seldom see later than December, is made by the opossum. This animal is evidently multiplying in the land, and is extending its range northward. Ten years ago they were rarely found here, and now they are very common. I hear that they are very abundant and troublesome on parts of Long Island. The hind foot of the opossum has a sort of thumb that opposes the other toes, and it is the imprint of this member that looks so strange. The under side of the foot is as naked as the human hand, and this adds to the novel look of the track in the snow.

Late in the fall, my hired man set a trap in a hole in hopes of catching a skunk, but instead he caught a possum by one of its fore feet. The poor thing was badly crippled, and he kept it in a barrel for a couple of weeks and fed it, to try and make amends for the injury he had done. Then he gave it its freedom, though the injured foot had healed but little.

Soon after he set his trap in the same hole, and to his annoyance caught the possum again, this time by one of the hind feet. He brought the quiet, uncomplaining creature to me by its prehensile tail, and asked me what should be done with or for it. I concluded to make a hospital for it in one corner of my study. I made it a nest behind a pile of magazines, and fed and nursed it for several weeks. It never made a sound, or showed the least uneasiness or sign of suffering, that I was aware of, in all that time. By day it slept curled up in its nest. If disturbed, it did not "play possum," that is, did not feign sleep or death, but opened its mouth and grinned up at you in a sort of comical, idiotic way. At night it hobbled about the study, and ate the meat and cake I had placed for it. Sometimes by day it would come out of the corner and eat food under the lounge, eating very much after the manner of a pig, though not so greedily. Indeed, all its motions were very slow, like those of the skunk.

The skin of the opossum is said to be so fetid that a dog will not touch it. A dog is always suspicious of an animal that shows no fear and makes no attempt to get out of his way. This fetidness of the opossum is not apparent to my sense.

After a while my patient began to be troublesome by climbing upon the book-shelves and inspecting the books, so I concluded to discharge him from the hospital. One night I carried him to the open door by his tail, put him down upon the door-sill, and told him to go forth. He hesitated, looked back into the warm room, then out into the winter night, then thought of his maimed feet, and of traps in holes where unsuspecting possums live, and could not reach a decision. "Come," I said, "I have done all I can for you; go forth and shift for yourself." Slowly, like a very old man, he climbed down out of the door and disappeared in the darkness. I have no doubt he regained his freedom with a sigh. It is highly probable that, if a trap is set in his way again, he will put his foot in it as innocently as before.

One day in March one of my neighbors brought to me a handful of young possums, very young, sixteen of them, like newly born mice. The mother had been picked up dead on the railroad, killed, as so often happens to coons, foxes, muskrats, and woodchucks, by the night express. The young were in her pouch, each clinging to its teat, dead. The young are carried and nursed by the mothers in this curious pocket till they are four or five weeks old, or of the size of large mice. After this she frequently carries them about, clinging to various parts of her body, some with their tails wound around hers.

The next winter, two or more possums and a skunk took up their quarters under my study floor. It was not altogether a happy family. Just what their disagreements were about, I do not know, but the skunk evidently tried to roast the possums out. The possums stood it better than I could. I came heartily to wish they were all roasted out. I was beginning to devise ways and means, when I think the skunk took himself off. After that, my only annoyance was from the quarreling of the possums among themselves, and their ceaseless fussing around under there, both day and night. At times they made sounds as if they were scratching matches on the under side of the floor: then they seemed to be remaking or shifting their beds from one side to the other. Sometimes I think they snored in their sleep. One night, as I was going from the house to the study, I heard a rustling in the dry leaves and grass, beside the path. Lighting a match, I approached the spot, and found one of the possums just setting out on his night's excursions. I stooped down and stroked his head and scratched his back, but he did not move; he only opened his mouth a little and looked silly.

XIII
WILD MICE

One of the prettiest and most abundant of our native mice is the deer mouse, also called the white-footed mouse; a very beautiful creature, nocturnal in his habits, with large ears, and large, fine eyes full of a wild, harmless look. He is daintily marked, with white feet and a white belly. When disturbed by day he is very easily captured, having none of the cunning or viciousness of the common Old World mouse. He is found in both fields and woods.

It is he who, high in the hollow trunk of some tree, lays by a store of beech-nuts for winter use. Every nut is carefully shelled, and the cavity that serves as storehouse lined with grass and leaves. The wood-chopper frequently squanders this precious store. I have seen half a peck taken from one tree, as clean and white as if put up by the most delicate hands,--as they were. How long it must have taken the little creature to collect this quantity, to hull them one by one, and convey them up to his fifth-story chamber!

But the deer mice do not always carry their supplies home in this manner; they often hide them in the nearest convenient place. I have known them to carry a pint or more of hickory nuts and deposit them in a pair of boots standing in the chamber of an outhouse. Near the chestnut-trees they will fill little pocket-like depressions in the ground with chestnuts; in a grain-field they carry the grain under stones; under some cover beneath cherry-trees they collect great numbers of cherry-pits. Hence, when cold weather comes, instead of staying at home like the chipmunk, they gad about hither and thither looking up their supplies. One may see their tracks on the snow everywhere in the woods and fields and by the roadside. The advantage of this way of living is that it leads to activity, and probably to sociability.

One day, on my walk in the woods, I saw at one point the mice-tracks unusually thick around a small sugar-maple. It was doubtless their granary; they had beech-nuts stored there, I'll warrant. There were two entrances to the cavity of the tree,--one at the base, and one seven or eight feet up. At the upper one, which was only just of the size of a mouse, a squirrel had been trying to break in. He had cut and chiseled the solid wood to the depth of nearly an inch, and his chips strewed the snow all about. He knew what was in there, and the mice knew that he knew; hence their apparent consternation. They had rushed wildly about over the snow, and, I doubt not, had given the piratical red squirrel a piece of their minds. A few yards away the mice had a hole down into the snow, which perhaps led to some snug den under the ground. Hither they may have been slyly removing their stores while the squirrel was at work with his back turned. One more night and he would effect an entrance: what a good joke upon him if he found the cavity empty! These native mice, I imagine, have to take many precautions to prevent their winter stores being plundered by the squirrels, who live, as it were, from hand to mouth.

The wild mice are fond of bees and of honey, and they apparently like nothing better than to be allowed to take up their quarters in winter in some vacant space in a hive of bees. A chamber just over the bees seems to be preferred, as here they get the benefit of the warmth generated by the insects. One very cold winter I wrapped up one of my hives with a shawl. Before long I noticed that the shawl was beginning to have a very torn and tattered appearance. On examination, I found that a native mouse had established itself in the top of the hive, and had levied a ruinous tax upon the shawl to make itself a nest. Never was a fabric more completely reduced into its original elements than were large sections of that shawl. It was a masterly piece of analysis. The work of the wheel and the loom was exactly reversed, and what was once shawl was now the finest and softest of wool.

The white-footed mouse is much more common along the fences and in the woods than one would suspect. One winter day I set a mouse-trap--the kind known as the delusion trap--beneath some ledges in the edge of the woods, to determine what species of mouse was most active at this season. The snow fell so deeply that I did not visit my trap for two or three weeks. When I did so, it was literally packed full of white-footed mice. There were seven in all, and not room for another. Our woods are full of these little creatures, and they appear to have a happy, social time of it, even in the severest winters. Their little tunnels under the snow and their hurried leaps upon its surface may be noted everywhere. They link tree and stump, or rock and tree, by their pretty trails. They evidently travel for adventure and to hear the news, as well as for food. They know that foxes and owls are about, and they keep pretty close to cover. When they cross an exposed place, they do it hurriedly.

The field or meadow mice doubtless welcome the snow. They can now come out of their dens in the ground or beneath the flat stones and lead a more free and active life. The snow is their friend. It keeps off the cold, and it shields their movements from the eyes of their enemies, the owls, hawks, and foxes. Now they can venture abroad from their retreats without fear. They make little tunnels and roadways everywhere over the surface of the ground. They build winter houses under the great drifts. They found little mouse colonies in places where they have never been in summer. The conditions of life with them are entirely changed. They can get at the roots of the grasses, or the various herbs and seeds they feed upon, as well as in the snowless seasons, and without exposure to their enemies.

I fancy they have great times there beneath the drifts. Maybe they have their picnics and holidays then as we have ours in summer. When the drifts disappear in spring, you may often see where they have had their little encampments: a few square yards of the pasture or meadow bottom will look as if a map had been traced upon it; tunnels and highways running and winding in every direction and connecting the nests of dry grass, which might stand for the cities and towns on the map. These runways are smooth and round like pipes, and only a little larger than the bodies of the mice. I think it is only the meadow field-mouse that lives in this way beneath the snow.

I met one of these mice in my travels one day under peculiar conditions. He was on his travels also, and we met in the middle of a mountain lake. I was casting my fly there, when I saw, just sketched or etched upon the glassy surface, a delicate V-shaped figure, the point of which reached about to the middle of the lake, while the two sides, as they diverged, faded out toward the shore. I saw the point of this V was being slowly pushed across the lake. I drew near in my boat, and beheld a little mouse swimming vigorously for the opposite shore. His little legs appeared like swiftly revolving wheels beneath him. As I came near, he dived under the water to escape me, but came up again like a cork and just as quickly. It was laughable to see him repeatedly duck beneath the surface and pop back again in a twinkling. He could not keep under water more than a second or two. Presently I reached him my oar, when he ran up it and into the palm of my hand, where he sat for some time and arranged his fur and warmed himself. He did not show the slightest fear. It was probably the first time he had ever shaken hands with a human being. He had doubtless lived all his life in the woods, and was strangely unsophisticated. How his little round eyes did shine, and how he sniffed me to find out if I was more danger-ous than I appeared to his sight!

After a while I put him down in the bottom of the boat and resumed my fish-ing. But it was not long before he became very restless, and evidently wanted to go about his business. He would climb up to the edge of the boat and peer down into the water. Finally he could brook the delay no longer and plunged boldly over-board; but he had either changed his mind or lost his reckoning, for he started back in the direction from which he had come, and the last I saw of him he was a mere speck vanishing in the shadows near the shore.

Later on I saw another mouse, while we were at work in the fields, that in-terested me also. This one was our native white-footed mouse. We disturbed the mother with her young in her nest, and she rushed out with her little ones clinging to her teats. A curious spectacle she presented as she rushed along, as if slit and torn into rags. Her pace was so hurried that two of the young could not keep their hold and were left in the weeds. We remained quiet, and presently the mother came back looking for them. When she had found one, she seized it as a cat seizes her kitten and made off with it. In a moment or two she came back and found the other one and carried it away. I was curious to see if the young would take hold of her teats again as at first, and be dragged away in that manner, but they did not. It would be interesting to know if they seize hold of their mother by instinct when danger threatens, or if they simply retain the hold which they already have. I believe the flight of the family always takes place in this manner with this species of mouse.

I suspect that our white-footed mouse is capable of lending a hand to a fellow in distress; at least, the following incident looks like it. One season they overran my cabin in the woods, and gave me a good deal of annoyance; so much so that I tried trapping them, using the ordinary circular trap with four or five holes and wire springs. One night I heard the trap spring in the attic over my head, followed by the kicking and straggling of the mouse. This continued for a few moments, when all was still. "There," I said, "that mouse is dead." Presently the rattling of the trap recommenced, and continued so long at short intervals that going to sleep was out of the question. I fancied the mouse was too strong for the trap, so I went upstairs to investigate. The captive was dead, sure enough, and I was more puzzled than ever. On examining him closely, I found the fur on his back was wet and much rumpled. I concluded, therefore, that his companions had seized him there, and had been tugging away at him to drag him out of the trap, causing the rattling I had heard. No other explanation seems probable.

The least mammal in our woods is the little mouse-like shrew, scarcely more than three inches long, tail and all. And it is the shyest and least known. One gets a glimpse of it only at rare intervals, while sitting or standing motionless in the woods. There is a slight rustle under the leaves, and you may see a tiny form dart across a little opening in the leafy carpet. Its one dread seems to be exposure to the light. If it were watched and waited for by a hundred enemies, it could hardly be more hurried and cautious in its movements. And when once captured and fairly exposed to the light, it soon dies, probably of fright. One night in midsummer, when I was camping in the woods, one of them got into an empty tin pail and was dead in the morning. A teacher caught one in a delusion trap, and attempted to take it to her school, to show her children, but it was dead when she got there. In winter it makes little tunnels under the snow in the woods, now and then coming to the surface, and, after a few jumps, diving under the snow again. Its tracks are like the most delicate stitching. I have never found its nest or seen its young. Like all the shrews, it lives mainly upon worms and insects.

The track of one of our native mice we do not see upon the snow,--that of the jumping mouse. So far as I know, it is the only one of our mice that hibernates. It is much more rare than its cousin the deer mouse, or white-footed mouse, and I have never known it to be found in barns or dwellings. I think I have heard it called the kangaroo mouse, because of its form and its manner of running, which is in long leaps. Its fore legs are small and short, and its hind legs long and strong. It bounds along, leaping two or more feet at a time. I used to see it when a boy, but have not met with one for many years.

One summer, a boy who lives in Dutchess County, across the Hudson from my house, caught four of these mice in a wire trap, two males and two females. The boy said that when he picked up the trap the two males fell dead, from fright he thought. One of the females died in October, but the other lived and began hibernating early in November. He took it to his teacher in New York, who kept it through the winter. She made a pocket for it in a woolen sock, but it was not suited with it, for in January it woke up and made itself a neat little blanket from the wool which it nibbled from the sock. In this it rolled itself and went to sleep again. A week or two later I was at the school, and the teacher showed me her sleeping mouse. It was rolled up in a ball, with its tail wrapped about its head. I held it in the palm of my hand. It seemed almost as cold as a dead mouse, and I could not see it breathe. It was carefully put back in its blanket.

Not long after this, a small house-mouse was put in the box with it. "It was the tiniest little mouse," says Miss Burt, "you ever saw. It cuddled in with the hibernator, who got up at once and took care of this baby. The baby struck out independently and burrowed in the sand, and stole some of the wool and feathers from hibernator to line his own nest. But the jumping mouse went in with him, enlarged the nest, and cuddled down to him. They were great friends. But the baby smelled dreadfully, as all house-mice do, and I took him out. Then the hibernator curled up again and went into winter quarters.

"When the warm weather came on, she uncurled and ate and drank. She preferred pecan nuts and shredded-wheat biscuit, and ate corn. I tried to tame her. I took a strong feather and played with her. At first she resisted and was frightened, but after a while she 'stood it,' and would even eat and clean herself while I scratched her with this feather. But she was always terribly frightened, when coming out of her day's sleep, if I began to play with her. After being thoroughly waked up, she did not mind it. She would let me smooth her with my finger, and she would smell of my finger and go on eating, keeping an eye out. Three times she had a perfect fit of fright, lying on her back, and kicking and trembling violently. On these occasions she made a scuttling noise or cry, and I thought each time she would die, so I grew more and more cautious about meddling with her. There was one interesting thing about it,--she rose from these fits and ate heartily, and cleaned herself with great unconcern. I was tempted to believe that she shammed dying.

"The most interesting thing I ever saw her do was to climb up on her glass of water, sit on the rim, and put both little paws down and scoop up a big double-handful of water and wash her face and head. She made her face very wet, just like a person washing his face. She ate sunflower seeds, and often kept one eye shut a long time on first waking up. After the apple-blossoms came, I kept her box supplied with flowers, such as apple-blossoms, cherry, spruce, maple, and so on. Also I kept her box disinfected, with plenty of good, fresh country dirt. But she stuck to the old wool and feathers, and the little piano-duster."

The mouse continued hibernating at intervals till May. One damp, chilly morning Miss Burt thought she would add to her pet's coverings, the creature seemed so cold to the touch. "Little by little, much of her bedding of wool had been removed, although she had a pretty good blanket of it left, and the feather duster over her, which she appropriated long ago. So I resolved to carry some bits of flannel to school and, when I went to her box to give her the extra clothing, again found her as you saw her, rolled up in a ball. I covered her carefully, wrapped her all up, and put her back. Later in the day I peeped in, and she was awake. In the afternoon I took her out in her little blanket and looked at her. She was asleep, but started up, and, seeing herself out of her box, put up her little paw in fright. She trembled violently, and I hastily returned her to her box, but before I could cover her she fell back dead of fright." Miss Burt adds: "I have had her put in alcohol. One tiny paw is raised imploringly, suggestive of the sensitive nerves that caused her death."

XIV
GLIMPSES OF WILD LIFE

So fond am I of seeing Nature reassert herself that I even found some compensation in the loss of my chickens that bright November night when some wild creature, coon or fox, swept two of them out of the evergreens, and their squawking as they were hurried across the lawn called me from my bed to shout good-by after them. It gave a new interest to the hen-roost, this sudden incursion of wild nature. I feel bound to caution the boys about disturbing the wild rabbits that in summer breed in my currant-patch, and in autumn seek refuge under my study floor. The occasional glimpses I get of them about the lawn in the dusk, their cotton tails twinkling in the dimness, afford me a genuine pleasure. I have seen the time when I would go a good way to shoot a partridge; but I would not have killed, if I could, the one that started out of the vines that cover my rustic porch, as I approached that side of the house one autumn morning. How much of the woods, and of the untamable spirit of wild nature, she brought to my very door! It was tonic and exhilarating to see her whirl away toward the vineyard. I also owe a moment's pleasure to the gray squirrel that, finding my summer-house in the line of his travels one summer day, ran through it and almost over my feet as I sat idling with a book.

I am sure my power of digestion was improved that cold winter morning when, just as we were sitting down to breakfast about sunrise, a red fox loped along in front of the window, looking neither to the right nor to the left, and disappeared amid the currant-bushes. What of the wild and the cunning did he not bring! His graceful form and motion were in my mind's eye all day. When you have seen a fox loping along in that way, you have seen the poetry there is in the canine tribe. It is to the eye what a flowing measure is to the mind, so easy, so buoyant; the furry creature drifting along like a large red thistledown, or like a plume borne by the wind. It is something to remember with pleasure, that a muskrat sought my door one December night when a cold wave was swooping down upon us. Was he seeking shelter, or had he lost his reckoning? The dogs cornered him in the very doorway, and set up a great hubbub. In the darkness, thinking it was a cat, I put my hand down to feel it. The creature skipped to the other corner of the doorway, hitting my hand with its cold, rope-like tail. Lighting a match, I had a glimpse of him sitting up on his haunches like a woodchuck, confronting his enemies. I rushed in for the lantern, with the hope of capturing him alive, but before I returned, the dogs, growing bold, had finished him.

I have had but one call from a coon, that I am aware of, and I fear we did not treat him with due hospitality. He took up his quarters for the day in a Norway spruce, the branches of which nearly brushed the house. I had noticed that the dog was very curious about that tree all the afternoon. After dinner his curiosity culminated in repeated loud and confident barking. Then I began an investigation, expecting to find a strange cat, or at most a red squirrel. But a moment's scrutiny revealed his coonship. Then how to capture him became the problem. A long pole was procured, and I sought to dislodge him from his hold. The skill with which he maintained himself amid the branches excited our admiration. But after a time he dropped lightly to the ground, not in the least disconcerted, and at once on his guard against both man and beast. The dog was a coward, and dared not face him. When the coon's attention was diverted, the dog would rush in; then one of us would attempt to seize the coon's tail, but he faced about so quickly, his black eyes gleaming, that the hand was timid about seizing him. But finally in his skirmishing with the dog I caught him by the tail, and bore him safely to an open flour-barrel, and he was our prisoner.

Much amusement my little boy and I anticipated with him. He partook of food that same day, and on the second day would eat the chestnuts in our presence. Never did he show the slightest fear of us or of anything, but he was unwearied in his efforts to regain his freedom. After a few days we put a strap upon his neck and kept him tethered by a chain. But in the night, by dint of some hocus-pocus, he got the chain unsnapped and made off, and he is now, I trust, a patriarch of his tribe, wearing a leather necktie.

The skunk visits every farm sooner or later. One night I came near shaking hands with one on my very door-stone. I thought it was the cat, and put down my hand to stroke it, when the creature, probably appreciating my mistake, moved off up the bank, revealing to me the white stripe on its body and the kind of cat I had saluted. The skunk is not easily ruffled, and seems to employ excellent judgment in the use of its terrible weapon.

Several times I have had calls from woodchucks. One looked in at the open door of my study one day, and, after sniffing a while, and not liking the smell of such clover as I was compelled to nibble there, moved on to better pastures. Another one invaded the kitchen door while we were at dinner. The dogs promptly challenged him, and there was a lively scrimmage upon the door-stone. I thought the dogs were fighting, and rushed to part them. The incident broke in upon the drowsy summer noon, as did the appearance of the muskrat upon the frigid December night.

The woodchuck episode that afforded us the most amusement occurred one midsummer. We were at work in a newly-planted vineyard, when the man with the cultivator saw, a few yards in front of him, some large gray object that at first puzzled him. He approached it, and found it to be an old woodchuck with a young one in her mouth. She was carrying her kitten as does a cat, by the nape of the neck. Evidently she was moving her family to pastures new. As the man was in the line of her march, she stopped and considered what was to be done. He called to me, and I approached slowly. As the mother saw me closing in on her flank, she was suddenly seized with a panic, and, dropping her young, she fled precipitately for the cover of a large pile of grape-posts some ten or twelve rods distant. We pursued hotly, and overhauled her as she was within one jump of the house of refuge. Taking her by the tail, I carried her back to her baby; but she heeded it not. It was only her own bacon now that she was solicitous about. The young one remained where he had been dropped, keeping up a brave, reassuring whistle that was in ludicrous contrast to his exposed and helpless condition. He was the smallest woodchuck I had ever seen, not much larger than a large rat. His head and shoulders were so large in proportion to the body as to give him a comical look. He could not walk about yet, and had never before been above ground. Every moment or two he would whistle cheerily, as the old one does when safe in his den with the farm-dog fiercely baying outside.

We took the youngster home, and my little boy was delighted over the prospect of a tame woodchuck. Not till the next day would he eat. Then, getting a taste of the milk, he clutched the spoon that held it with great eagerness, and sucked away like a little pig. We were all immensely diverted by him. He ate eagerly, grew rapidly, and was soon able to run about.

As the old one had been killed, we became curious as to the fate of the rest of her family, for no doubt there were more. Had she moved them, or had we intercepted her on her first trip? We knew where the old den was, but not the new. So we would keep a lookout. Near the end of the week, on passing by the old den, there were three young ones creeping about a few feet from its mouth. They were starved out, and had come forth to see what could be found. We captured them all, and the young family was again united. How these poor, half-famished creatures did lay hold of the spoon when they got a taste of the milk! One could not help laughing. Their little shining black paws were so handy and so smooth; they seemed as if encased in kid gloves. The captives throve well upon milk, and then upon milk and clover.

But after the novelty of the thing had worn off, the boy found he had incumbered himself with serious duties in assuming the position of foster-mother to this large family; so he gave them all away but one, the first one captured, which had outstripped all the others in growth. This soon became a very amusing pet, but he always protested when handled, and always objected to confinement. I should mention that the cat had a kitten about the age of the chuck, and, as she had more milk than the kitten could dispose of, the chuck, when we first got him, was often placed in the nest with the kitten, and was regarded by the cat as tenderly as her own, and allowed to nurse freely. Thus a friendship sprang up between the kitten and the woodchuck, which lasted as long as the latter lived. They would play together precisely like two kittens,--clinch and tumble about and roll upon the grass in a very amusing way. Finally the woodchuck took up his abode under the floor of the kitchen, and gradually relapsed into a half-wild state. He would permit no familiarities from any one save the kitten, but each day they would have a turn or two at their old games of rough-and-tumble. The chuck was now over half grown, and procured his own living. One day the dog, who had all along looked upon him with a jealous eye, encountered him too far from cover, and his career ended then and there.

In July the woodchuck was forgotten in our interest in a little gray rabbit which we found nearly famished. It was so small that it could sit in the hollow of one's hand. Some accident had probably befallen its mother. The tiny creature looked spiritless and forlorn. We had to force the milk into its mouth. But in a day or two it began to revive, and would lap the milk eagerly. Soon it took to grass and clover, and then to nibbling sweet apples and early pears. It grew rapidly, and was one of the softest and most harmless-looking pets I had ever seen. For a month or more the little rabbit was the only company I had, and it helped to beguile the time immensely. In coming in from the field or from my work, I seldom failed to bring it a handful of red clover blossoms, of which it became very fond. One day it fell slyly to licking my hand, and I discovered it wanted salt. I would then moisten my fingers, dip them into the salt, and offer them to the rabbit. How rapidly the delicate little tongue would play upon them, darting out to the right and left of the large front incisors, the slender paws being pressed against my hand as if to detain it!

But the rabbit proved really untamable; its wild nature could not be overcome. In its large box-cage or prison, where it could see nothing but the tree above it, it was tame, and would at times frisk playfully about my hand and strike it gently with its forefeet; but the moment it was liberated in a room, or let down in the grass with a string about its neck, all its wild nature came forth. In the room it would run and hide; in the open it would make desperate efforts to escape, and leap and bound as you drew in the string that held it. At night, too, it never failed to try to make its escape from the cage, and finally, when two thirds grown, it succeeded, and we saw it no more.

XV
A LIFE OF FEAR

As I sat looking from my window the other morning upon a red squirrel gathering nuts from a small hickory, and storing them up in his den in the bank, I was forcibly reminded of the state of constant fear and apprehension in which the wild creatures live, and I tried to picture to myself what life would be to me, or to any of us, hedged about by so many dangers, real or imaginary.

The squirrel would shoot up the tree, making only a brown streak from the bottom to the top; would seize his nut and rush down again in the most hurried manner. Half way to his den, which was not over three rods distant, he would rush up the trunk of another tree for a few yards to make an observation. No danger being near, he would dive into his den and reappear again in a twinkling.

Returning for another nut, he would mount the second tree again for another observation. Satisfied that the coast was clear, he would spin along the top of the ground to the tree that bore the nuts, shoot up it as before, seize the fruit, and then back again to his retreat.

Never did he fail during the half hour or more that I watched him to take an observation on his way both to and from his nest. It was "snatch and run" with him. Something seemed to say to him all the time: "Look out! look out!" "The cat!" "The hawk!" "The owl!" "The boy with the gun!"

It was a bleak December morning; the first fine flakes of a cold, driving snowstorm were just beginning to sift down, and the squirrel was eager to finish harvesting his nuts in time. It was quite touching to see how hurried and anxious and nervous he was. I felt like going out and lending a hand. The nuts were small, poor pig-nuts, and I thought of all the gnawing he would have to do to get at the scanty meat they held. My little boy once took pity on a squirrel that lived in the wall near the gate, and cracked the nuts for him, and put them upon a small board shelf in the tree where he could sit and eat them at his ease.

The red squirrel is not so provident as the chipmunk. He lays up stores irregularly, by fits and starts; he never has enough put up to carry him over the winter; hence he is more or less active all the season. Long before the December snow, the chipmunk has for days been making hourly trips to his den with full pockets of nuts or corn or buckwheat, till his bin holds enough to carry him through to April. He need not, and I believe does not, set foot out of doors during the whole winter. But the red squirrel trusts more to luck.

As alert and watchful as the red squirrel is, he is frequently caught by the cat. My Nig, as black as ebony, knows well the taste of his flesh. I have known him to be caught by the black snake and successfully swallowed. The snake, no doubt, lay in ambush for him.

This fear, this ever-present source of danger of the wild creatures, we know little about. Probably the only person in the civilized countries who is no better off than the animals in this respect is the Czar of Russia. He would not even dare gather nuts as openly as my squirrel. A blacker and more terrible cat than Nig would be lying in wait for him and would make a meal of him. The early settlers in this country must have experienced something of this dread of apprehension from the Indians. Many African tribes now live in the same state of constant fear of the slave-catchers or of other hostile tribes. Our ancestors, back in prehistoric times, must have known fear as a constant feeling. Hence the prominence of fear in infants and children when compared with the youth or the grown person. Babies are nearly always afraid of strangers.

In the domestic animals also, fear is much more active in the young than in the old. Nearly every farm boy has seen a calf but a day or two old, which its mother has secreted in the woods or in a remote field, charge upon him furiously with a wild bleat, when first discovered. After this first ebullition of fear, it usually settles down into the tame humdrum of its bovine elders.

Eternal vigilance is the price of life with most of the wild creatures. There is only one among them whose wildness I cannot understand, and that is the common water turtle. Why is this creature so fearful? What are its enemies? I know of nothing that preys upon it. Yet see how watchful and suspicious these turtles are as they sun themselves upon a log or a rock. While you are yet many yards away from them, they slide down into the water and are gone.

The land turtle, on the other hand, shows scarcely a trace of fear. He will indeed pause in his walk when you are very near him, but he will not retreat into his shell till you have poked him with your foot or your cane. He appears to have no enemies; but the little spotted water turtle is as shy as if he were the delicate tidbit that every creature was searching for. I did once find one which a fox had dug out of the mud in winter, and carried a few rods and dropped on the snow, as if he had found he had no use for it.

One can understand the fearlessness of the skunk. Nearly every creature but the farm-dog yields to him the right of way. All dread his terrible weapon. If you meet one in your walk in the twilight fields, the chances are that you will turn out for him, not he for you. He may even pursue you, just for the fun of seeing you run. He comes waltzing toward you, apparently in the most hilarious spirits.

The coon is probably the most courageous creature among our familiar wild animals. Who ever saw a coon show the white feather? He will face any odds with perfect composure. I have seen a coon upon the ground, beset by four men and two dogs, and never for a moment losing his presence of mind, or showing a sign of fear. The raccoon is clear grit.

The fox is a very wild and suspicious creature, but curiously enough, when you suddenly come face to face with him, when he is held by a trap, or driven by the hound, his expression is not that of fear, but of shame and guilt. He seems to diminish in size and to be overwhelmed with humiliation. Does he know himself to be an old thief, and is that the reason of his embarrassment? The fox has no enemies but man, and when he is fairly outwitted he looks the shame he evidently feels.

In the heart of the rabbit fear constantly abides. How her eyes protrude! She can see back and forward and on all sides as well as a bird. The fox is after her, the owls are after her, the gunners are after her, and she has no defense but her speed. She always keeps well to cover. The northern hare keeps in the thickest brush. If the hare or rabbit crosses a broad open exposure it does so hurriedly, like a mouse when it crosses the road. The mouse is in danger of being pounced upon by a hawk, and the hare or rabbit by the snowy owl, or else the great horned owl.

A friend of mine was following one morning a fresh rabbit track through an open field. Suddenly the track came to an end, as if the creature had taken wings,--as it had after an unpleasant fashion. There, on either side of its last foot imprint, were several parallel lines in the snow, made by the wings of the great owl that had swooped down and carried it off. What a little tragedy was seen written there upon the white, even surface of the field!

The rabbit has not much wit. Once, when a boy, I saw one that had been recently caught, liberated in an open field in the presence of a dog that was being held a few yards away. The poor thing lost all presence of mind, and was quickly caught by the clumsy dog.

A hunter once saw a hare running upon the ice along the shore of one of the Rangeley lakes. Presently a lynx appeared in hot pursuit; as soon as the hare found it was being pursued, it began to circle, foolish thing. This gave the lynx greatly the advantage, as it could follow in a much smaller circle. Soon the hare was run down and seized.

I saw a similar experiment tried with a red squirrel with quite opposite results. The boy who had caught the squirrel in his wire trap had a very bright and nimble dog about the size of a fox, that seemed to be very sure he could catch a red squirrel under any circumstances if only the trees were out of the way. So the boy went to the middle of an open field with his caged squirrel, the dog, who seemed to know what was up, dancing and jumping about him. It was in midwinter; the snow had a firm crust that held boy and dog alike. The dog was drawn back a few yards and the squirrel liberated.

Then began one of the most exciting races I have witnessed for a long time. It was impossible for the lookers-on not to be convulsed with laughter, though neither dog nor squirrel seemed to regard the matter as much of a joke. The squirrel had all his wits about him, and kept them ready for instant use. He did not show the slightest confusion. He was no match for the dog in fair running, and he discovered this fact in less than three seconds; he must win, if at all, by strategy. Not a straight course for the nearest tree, but a zigzag course, yea, a double or treble zigzag course. Every instant the dog was sure the squirrel was his, and every instant he was disappointed. It was incredible and bewildering to him. The squirrel dodged this way and that. The dog looked astonished and vexed. Then the squirrel issued from between his enemy's hind legs and made three jumps towards the woods before he was discovered. Our sides ached with laughter, cruel as it may seem.

It was evident the squirrel would win. The dog seemed to redouble his efforts. He would overshoot the game, or shoot by it to the right or left. The squirrel was the smaller craft, and could out-tack him easily. One more leap and the squirrel was up a tree, and the dog was overwhelmed with confusion and disgust. He could not believe his senses. "Not catch a squirrel in such a field as that? Go to, I will have him yet!" and he bounded up the tree as high as one's head, and then bit the bark of it in his anger and chagrin.

The boy says his dog has never bragged since about catching red squirrels "if only the trees were out of reach!"

When any of the winged creatures are engaged in a life and death race in that way, or in any other race, the tactics of the squirrel do not work; the pursuer never overshoots nor shoots by his mark. The flight of the two is timed as if they were parts of one whole. A hawk will pursue a sparrow or a robin through a zigzag course and not lose a stroke or half a stroke of the wing by reason of any darting to the right or left. The clue is held with fatal precision. No matter how quickly nor how often the sparrow or the finch changes its course, its enemy changes, simultaneously, as if every move was known to it from the first.

The same thing may be noticed among the birds in their love chasings; the pursuer seems to know perfectly the mind of the pursued. This concert of action among birds is very curious. When they are on the alert, a flock of sparrows, or pigeons, or cedar-birds, or snow buntings, or blackbirds, will all take flight as if there were but one bird, instead of a hundred. The same impulse seizes every individual bird at the same instant, as if they were sprung by electricity.

Or when a flock of birds is in flight, it is still one body, one will; it will rise, or circle, or swoop with a unity that is truly astonishing.

A flock of snow buntings will perform their aerial evolutions with a precision that the best-trained soldiery cannot equal. Have the birds an extra sense which we have not? A brood of young partridges in the woods will start up like an explosion, every brown particle and fragment hurled into the air at the same instant. Without word or signal, how is it done?

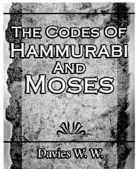

The Codes Of Hammurabi And Moses
W. W. Davies

QTY

The discovery of the Hammurabi Code is one of the greatest achievements of archaeology, and is of paramount interest, not only to the student of the Bible, but also to all those interested in ancient history...

Religion   **ISBN:** *1-59462-338-4*   **Pages:132**
MSRP $12.95

The Theory of Moral Sentiments
Adam Smith

QTY

This work from 1749. contains original theories of conscience amd moral judgment and it is the foundation for systemof morals.

Philosophy **ISBN:** *1-59462-777-0*   **Pages:536**
MSRP $19.95

Jessica's First Prayer
Hesba Stretton

QTY

In a screened and secluded corner of one of the many railway-bridges which span the streets of London there could be seen a few years ago, from five o'clock every morning until half past eight, a tidily set-out coffee-stall, consisting of a trestle and board, upon which stood two large tin cans, with a small fire of charcoal burning under each so as to keep the coffee boiling during the early hours of the morning when the work-people were thronging into the city on their way to their daily toil...

Pages:84

Childrens   **ISBN:** *1-59462-373-2*   *MSRP $9.95*

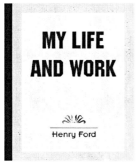

My Life and Work
Henry Ford

QTY

Henry Ford revolutionized the world with his implementation of mass production for the Model T automobile. Gain valuable business insight into his life and work with his own auto-biography... "We have only started on our development of our country we have not as yet, with all our talk of wonderful progress, done more than scratch the surface. The progress has been wonderful enough but..."

Pages:300

Biographies/   **ISBN:** *1-59462-198-5*   *MSRP $21.95* www.bookjungle.com *email: sales@bookjungle.com fax: 630-214-0564 mail: Book Jungle PO Box 2226 Champaign, IL 61825*

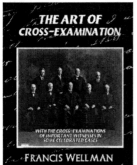

The Art of Cross-Examination
Francis Wellman

QTY

I presume it is the experience of every author, after his first book is published upon an important subject, to be almost overwhelmed with a wealth of ideas and illustrations which could readily have been included in his book, and which to his own mind, at least, seem to make a second edition inevitable. Such certainly was the case with me; and when the first edition had reached its sixth impression in five months, I rejoiced to learn that it seemed to my publishers that the book had met with a sufficiently favorable reception to justify a second and considerably enlarged edition. ..

Pages:412

Reference   ISBN: *1-59462-647-2*   *MSRP $19.95*

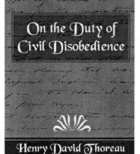

On the Duty of Civil Disobedience
Henry David Thoreau

QTY

Thoreau wrote his famous essay, On the Duty of Civil Disobedience, as a protest against an unjust but popular war and the immoral but popular institution of slave-owning. He did more than write—he declined to pay his taxes, and was hauled off to gaol in consequence. Who can say how much this refusal of his hastened the end of the war and of slavery ?

Law   ISBN: *1-59462-747-9*   **Pages:48**
                                             MSRP $7.45

Dream Psychology Psychoanalysis for Beginners
Sigmund Freud

QTY

Sigmund Freud, born Sigismund Schlomo Freud (May 6, 1856 - September 23, 1939), was a Jewish-Austrian neurologist and psychiatrist who co-founded the psychoanalytic school of psychology. Freud is best known for his theories of the unconscious mind, especially involving the mechanism of repression; his redefinition of sexual desire as mobile and directed towards a wide variety of objects; and his therapeutic techniques, especially his understanding of transference in the therapeutic relationship and the presumed value of dreams as sources of insight into unconscious desires.

Pages:196

Psychology   ISBN: *1-59462-905-6*   *MSRP $15.45*

The Miracle of Right Thought
Orison Swett Marden

QTY

Believe with all of your heart that you will do what you were made to do. When the mind has once formed the habit of holding cheerful, happy, prosperous pictures, it will not be easy to form the opposite habit. It does not matter how improbable or how far away this realization may see, or how dark the prospects may be, if we visualize them as best we can, as vividly as possible, hold tenaciously to them and vigorously struggle to attain them, they will gradually become actualized, realized in the life. But a desire, a longing without endeavor, a yearning abandoned or held indifferently will vanish without realization.

Pages:360

Self Help   ISBN: *1-59462-644-8*   *MSRP $25.45*

The Rosicrucian Cosmo-Conception Mystic Christianity *by Max Heindel* ISBN: *1-59462-188-8* **$38.95**
The Rosicrucian Cosmo-conception is not dogmatic, neither does it appeal to any other authority than the reason of the student. It is: not controversial, but is: sent forth in the, hope that it may help to clear... New Age/Religion Pages 646

Abandonment To Divine Providence *by Jean-Pierre de Caussade* ISBN: *1-59462-228-0* **$25.95**
"The Rev. Jean Pierre de Caussade was one of the most remarkable spiritual writers of the Society of Jesus in France in the 18th Century. His death took place at Toulouse in 1751. His works have gone through many editions and have been republished... Inspirational/Religion Pages 400

Mental Chemistry *by Charles Haanel* ISBN: *1-59462-192-6* **$23.95**
Mental Chemistry allows the change of material conditions by combining and appropriately utilizing the power of the mind. Much like applied chemistry creates something new and unique out of careful combinations of chemicals the mastery of mental chemistry... New Age Pages 354

The Letters of Robert Browning and Elizabeth Barret Barrett 1845-1846 vol II ISBN: *1-59462-193-4* **$35.95**
by Robert Browning and Elizabeth Barrett Biographies Pages 596

Gleanings In Genesis (volume I) *by Arthur W. Pink* ISBN: *1-59462-130-6* **$27.45**
Appropriately has Genesis been termed "the seed plot of the Bible" for in it we have, in germ form, almost all of the great doctrines which are afterwards fully developed in the books of Scripture which follow... Religion/Inspirational Pages 420

The Master Key *by L. W. de Laurence* ISBN: *1-59462-001-6* **$30.95**
In no branch of human knowledge has there been a more lively increase of the spirit of research during the past few years than in the study of Psychology, Concentration and Mental Discipline. The requests for authentic lessons in Thought Control, Mental Discipline and... New Age/Business Pages 422

The Lesser Key Of Solomon Goetia *by L. W. de Laurence* ISBN: *1-59462-092-X* **$9.95**
This translation of the first book of the "Lernegton" which is now for the first time made accessible to students of Talismanic Magic was done, after careful collation and edition, from numerous Ancient Manuscripts in Hebrew, Latin, and French... New Age/Occult Pages 92

Rubaiyat Of Omar Khayyam *by Edward Fitzgerald* ISBN:*1-59462-332-5* **$13.95**
Edward Fitzgerald, whom the world has already learned, in spite of his own efforts to remain within the shadow of anonymity, to look upon as one of the rarest poets of the century, was born at Bredfield, in Suffolk, on the 31st of March, 1809. He was the third son of John Purcell... Music Pages 172

Ancient Law *by Henry Maine* ISBN: *1-59462-128-4* **$29.95**
The chief object of the following pages is to indicate some of the earliest ideas of mankind, as they are reflected in Ancient Law, and to point out the relation of those ideas to modern thought. Religion/History Pages 452

Far-Away Stories *by William J. Locke* ISBN: *1-59462-129-2* **$19.45**
"Good wine needs no bush, but a collection of mixed vintages does. And this book is just such a collection. Some of the stories I do not want to remain buried for ever in the museum files of dead magazine-numbers an author's not unpardonable vanity..." Fiction Pages 272

Life of David Crockett *by David Crockett* ISBN: *1-59462-250-7* **$27.45**
"Colonel David Crockett was one of the most remarkable men of the times in which he lived. Born in humble life, but gifted with a strong will, an indomitable courage, and unremitting perseverance... Biographies/New Age Pages 424

Lip-Reading *by Edward Nitchie* ISBN: *1-59462-206-X* **$25.95**
Edward B. Nitchie, founder of the New York School for the Hard of Hearing, now the Nitchie School of Lip-Reading, Inc, wrote "LIP-READING Principles and Practice". The development and perfecting of this meritorious work on lip-reading was an undertaking... How-to Pages 400

A Handbook of Suggestive Therapeutics, Applied Hypnotism, Psychic Science ISBN: *1-59462-214-0* **$24.95**
by Henry Munro Health/New Age/Health/Self-help Pages 376

A Doll's House: and Two Other Plays *by Henrik Ibsen* ISBN: *1-59462-112-8* **$19.95**
Henrik Ibsen created this classic when in revolutionary 1848 Rome. Introducing some striking concepts in playwriting for the realist genre, this play has been studied the world over. Fiction/Classics/Plays 308

The Light of Asia *by sir Edwin Arnold* ISBN: *1-59462-204-3* **$13.95**
In this poetic masterpiece, Edwin Arnold describes the life and teachings of Buddha. The man who was to become known as Buddha to the world was born as Prince Gautama of India but he rejected the worldly riches and abandoned the reigns of power when... Religion/History/Biographies Pages 170

The Complete Works of Guy de Maupassant *by Guy de Maupassant* ISBN: *1-59462-157-8* **$16.95**
"For days and days, nights and nights, I had dreamed of that first kiss which was to consecrate our engagement, and I knew not on what spot I should put my lips..." Fiction/Classics Pages 240

The Art of Cross-Examination *by Francis L. Wellman* ISBN: *1-59462-309-0* **$26.95**
Written by a renowned trial lawyer, Wellman imparts his experience and uses case studies to explain how to use psychology to extract desired information through questioning. How-to/Science Reference Pages 408

Answered or Unanswered? *by Louisa Vaughan* ISBN: *1-59462-248-5* **$10.95**
Miracles of Faith in China Religion Pages 112

The Edinburgh Lectures on Mental Science (1909) *by Thomas* ISBN: *1-59462-008-3* **$11.95**
This book contains the substance of a course of lectures recently given by the writer in the Queen Street Hall, Edinburgh. Its purpose is to indicate the Natural Principles governing the relation between Mental Action and Material Conditions... New Age/Psychology Pages 148

Ayesha *by H. Rider Haggard* ISBN: *1-59462-301-5* **$24.95**
Verily and indeed it is the unexpected that happens! Probably if there was one person upon the earth from whom the Editor of this, and of a certain previous history, did not expect to hear again... Classics Pages 380

Ayala's Angel *by Anthony Trollope* ISBN: *1-59462-352-X* **$29.95**
The two girls were both pretty, but Lucy who was twenty-one who supposed to be simple and comparatively unattractive, whereas Ayala was credited, as her Bombwhat romantic name might show, with poetic charm and a taste for romance. Ayala when her father died was nineteen... Fiction Pages 484

The American Commonwealth *by James Bryce* ISBN: *1-59462-286-8* **$34.45**
An interpretation of American democratic political theory. It examines political mechanics and society from the perspective of Scotsman James Bryce Politics Pages 572

Stories of the Pilgrims *by Margaret P. Pumphrey* ISBN: *1-59462-116-0* **$17.95**
This book explores pilgrims religious oppression in England as well as their escape to Holland and eventual crossing to America on the Mayflower, and their early days in New England... History Pages 268

QTY

The Fasting Cure *by Sinclair Upton*   ISBN: *1-59462-222-1*   **$13.95**
In the Cosmopolitan Magazine for May, 1910, and in the Contemporary Review (London) for April, 1910, I published an article dealing with my experiences in fasting. I have written a great many magazine articles, but never one which attracted so much attention... New Age/Self Help/Health Pages 164

Hebrew Astrology *by Sepharial*   ISBN: *1-59462-308-2*   **$13.45**
In these days of advanced thinking it is a matter of common observation that we have left many of the old landmarks behind and that we are now pressing forward to greater heights and to a wider horizon than that which represented the mind-content of our progenitors... Astrology Pages 144

Thought Vibration or The Law of Attraction in the Thought World   ISBN: *1-59462-127-6*   **$12.95**
by William Walker Atkinson   Psychology/Religion Pages 144

Optimism *by Helen Keller*   ISBN: *1-59462-108-X*   **$15.95**
Helen Keller was blind, deaf, and mute since 19 months old, yet famously learned how to overcome these handicaps, communicate with the world, and spread her lectures promoting optimism. An inspiring read for everyone... Biographies/Inspirational Pages 84

Sara Crewe *by Frances Burnett*   ISBN: *1-59462-360-0*   **$9.45**
In the first place, Miss Minchin lived in London. Her home was a large, dull, tall one, in a large, dull square, where all the houses were alike, and all the sparrows were alike, and where all the door-knockers made the same heavy sound... Childrens/Classic Pages 88

The Autobiography of Benjamin Franklin *by Benjamin Franklin*   ISBN: *1-59462-135-7*   **$24.95**
The Autobiography of Benjamin Franklin has probably been more extensively read than any other American historical work, and no other book of its kind has had such ups and downs of fortune. Franklin lived for many years in England, where he was agent... Biographies/History Pages 332

Name	
Email	
Telephone	
Address	
City, State ZIP	

☐ **Credit Card**   ☐ **Check / Money Order**

Credit Card Number	
Expiration Date	
Signature	

Please Mail to: Book Jungle
PO Box 2226
Champaign, IL 61825
or Fax to: 630-214-0564

ORDERING INFORMATION
web: *www.bookjungle.com*
email: *sales@bookjungle.com*
fax: *630-214-0564*
mail: *Book Jungle PO Box 2226 Champaign, IL 61825*
or PayPal *to sales@bookjungle.com*

Please contact us for bulk discounts

DIRECT-ORDER TERMS

**20% Discount if You Order
Two or More Books**
Free Domestic Shipping!
Accepted: Master Card, Visa,
Discover, American Express

LaVergne, TN USA
24 May 2010
183788LV00004B/67/P